The Southern Cross

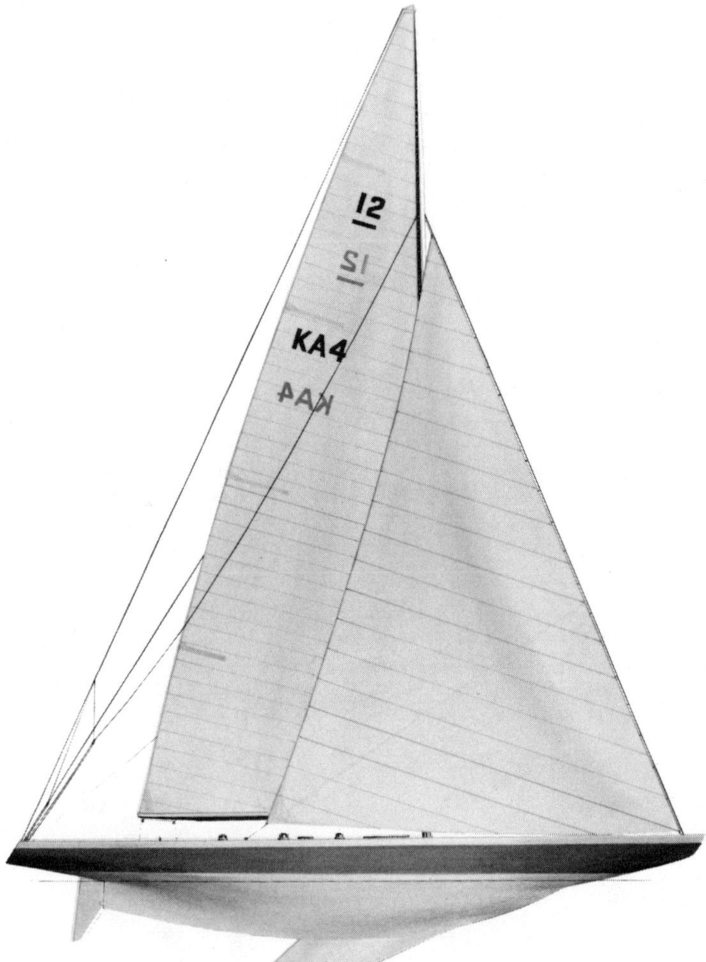

SOUTHERN CROSS
Royal Perth Yacht Club of Western Australia

Australia's 1974 challenge for America's Cup

THE SOUTHERN CROSS

Hugh D. Whall

Illustrations by Melbourne Smith

ADMIRALTY PUBLISHING HOUSE, LTD.
Annapolis, Maryland

 LIBRARY OF CONGRESS CATALOG NO. 74-78725
INTERNATIONAL STANDARD BOOK NO. 0-913544-04-3
Printed in the United States of America

For S.M.B.

Foreword

The story of the America's cup began a hundred and twenty-three years ago, almost exactly in the middle of the short span of a dozen years that was the heyday of the extreme clipper ships. These were years when speed under sail was of consuming interest not only to ship designers and builders, but also to business men, shop keepers, dray drivers — the man in the street. It was an age of lofty spars and ships with such beautifully rolling names as *Witch of the Wave, Staghound, Herald of the Morning.*

In England, it also was the age of flowering for yachting. With almost two centuries behind them since King Charles II brought the sport to England on his return from Holland in 1660, yachting was a pastime reserved for kings, nobility, and the leisured upper classes. King Charles, sometimes charged with being frivolous, was reputed to have had thirty yachts built in his twenty-five year reign,. and English yachtsmen were smug in their belief that they had no peers anywhere in the world when it came to pleasure craft.

Across the Atlantic, though, in what Englishmen persisted in calling the Colonies, yachting had an equally long heritage stemming largely from the interests of the Dutch patroons in early 1600 New York, but in nowise was there the quantity since the young nation was a while in developing the men of leisure class with the time and money for the sport. But by the middle of the nineteenth century, they, too, had appeared and in 1844 at a meeting aboard John Cox Stevens' 51-foot schooner-yacht *Gimcrack,* anchored off the Battery in New York City, the New York Yacht Club was founded. The same year the first, or so she was regarded generally, of the extreme clipper ships, the *Rainbow* was laid down, and it was only ten years later that the *Sovereign of the Seas* reputedly reached speeds of 22 knots on a passage out from London to Sydney.

Speed was nearly a world passion, fanned by often extravagant reports in the world press, and it involved not only the clippers, but the work-a-day longshore craft and yachts as well. It was of particular concern to English yachtsmen, and American as well. In England, early rating rules had their effect, too, and the designs developed were long, narrow and deep – known to the English as "out-and-outers" but elsewhere in the world as "plank-on-edge" boats. In America, on the other hand, design interest was more pragmatic and followed the development of the fast packet schooners that plied the coasts carrying mail, passengers and express freight, as well as the pilot schooners, which relied heavily on speed since it was the first pilot to meet an incoming ship that normally got the job of bringing her in. The pilot and packet schooner designs were relatively broad in beam and shallow in draft, and in general diametrically the opposite pole from the English design. The English considered them completely outré, but until 1851 there had been no international sailing contests and the twain seemingly were destined never to meet.

Then in that year, the Great International Exhibition,

the first World's Fair, was built in Hyde Park in London with Queen Victoria's consort, Prince Albert, as the director. With that in the offing, John Cox Stevens, still commodore of the then not yet venerable New York Yacht Club, proposed to a group of five fellow club members, including two other founding members, that they build a schooner, sail her to England, and take the measure of England's plank-on-edge craft. The gentlemen of leisure agreed, and George Steers, who at the age of 31 was something of a boy wonder of schooner designers as well as a sometime protege of the commodore, was commissioned to design a 170-ton schooner and to supervise her building in the yards of William H. Brown on New York's East River. Steers had designed the commodore's *Gimcrack* but some years earlier also had built a racing shell that he had named after his mentor.

The schooner's contract price was $30,000, ready for sea and subject to her demonstrating she was the fastest schooner afloat in America, but because of delays in building and in her trials and because of what looked like some suspiciously sharp dealing on the part of the syndicate, Steers eventually turned her over to her owners for $20,000, still a princely sum in the days when a dollar a day was a prime wage.

Launched as the *America,* the schooner was made ready and the syndicate hired Richard "Old Dick" Brown, owner of the *Mary Taylor,* a highly successful pilot schooner also from a Steers model, as skipper. With designer George Steers aboard as well as his older brother, James, and two teen-aged nephews, the *America* departed New York for Le Havre where she was to be put in racing trim. She made the voyage in twenty days, six hours, despite having been becalmed for a bit over five days in mid passage. Refitted, she proceeded to Cowes and as she approached port was drawn into a brush with the 80-ton cutter *Lavrock,* a new boat that was regarded by the

British as the fastest in the fleet and rated equal to schooners of the *America's* tonnage. The brush was carefully calculated because while the English had no doubts their boats were without compare, still they looked forward to solid proof.

Starting from astern, the *America* worked out to windward of the cutter, passed her easily and in four miles had left her a half-mile astern. Word of the results flashed through the fleet, and the shocked Englishmen developed a mass tactic of ignoring the *America.* While they socially wined and dined the visiting crew in impeccable hospitality, none would agree to meet the *America* on the race course, despite Commodore Stevens' straight challenge that included an offer to cover all bets up to $50,000. (There is little doubt that the syndicate had in mind recovering the costs of the schooner and her campaign, as well as a handsome profit, in winning wagers, a practice that was more common in yachting then than it is today.)

But there were no takers. Even the staid "London Times" castigated the yachtsmen for ignoring the challenge, likened them to wood pigeons and skylarks huddling on the ground as a sparrowhawk appears on the horizon, and questioned their "pith and courage."

Under such a barrage and despite some attempt to rule her out, the *America* was invited to take part in a fleet race around the Isle of Wight for "The Royal Yacht Squadron's One Hundred Guinea Cup" which squadron members had voted early in 1851, specifying that the race was open to "all rigs and all nations" as part of the Fair activities. The *America* was the only foreign yacht to enter the fleet that finally started which included six other schooners and eight cutters.

The story of that 45-mile race, which the *America* won with ease, has been told, re-told and mis-told in the years since, and in the process has developed myths and legends by the score. But there is little question that the most accurate account was contained in two dispatches carried by the Times following the race on August 22 and 23, 1851, which Charles Boswell recovered for his carefully documented story of the famous yacht, "The America," some years ago. The name of the Times' correspondent has gone unrecorded but it was clear from his report that he was both knowledgeable and experienced in yachting reporting.

Perhaps the most persistent myth was one that Commodore Stevens himself apparently started shortly after returning from England, which concerned an interchange between Queen Victoria and her Signal Master as the royal steam-yacht *Victoria and Albert* lay at the finish line. According to the story, the Queen queried her signalman on the progress of the yachts to be told *America* was first, and on her question as to who was second, the reply reputedly was:

"Ah, Your Majesty, there is no second."

Reading the Times report, that myth — graphic as it may be — had no foundation because the Queen had returned to Osbourn House, the summer palace just east of Cowes, long before *America* finished at 8:37 p.m. Conceivably, the exchange could have occurred as the *Victoria and Albert* lay off Alum Bay at the mouth of the Solent some two-and-a-half hours earlier to watch as the *America* rounded the Needles into the last leg of the course. At that point, the *America's* closest competitor, the cutter *Aurora,* was some seven-and-a-half miles astern. But most probably it was an embellishment of a paragraph in the Times report which read:

"Off Cowes were innumerable yachts, and on every side was heard the hail, 'Is the *America* first?' — The answer, 'Yes.' 'What's second?' — The reply, 'Nothing'."

But even that is open to some question since the *America's* 15-mile run from the Needles to the finish had been painfully slow with little wind and that fitful. Behind her, though, the *Aurora,* at 47-tons one of the smallest boats in the fleet, had come up the Solent on the edge of the night breeze and actually finished only eight minutes behind the *America* at 8:45. Had the finish been two-and-a-half miles farther, there may well have been no cup for *America.*

The *America's* win confirmed the fears English yachtsmen had acquired after the first brush and despite repeated challenges from Commodore Stevens, only one race for a wager of a hundred pounds was arranged with the 100-ton, iron-hulled schooner *Titania,* which the *America* also drubbed unmercifully. The syndicate members, in some disgust over the lack of action, put the *America* up for sale and she was purchased a month later by a young British army officer, Captain John de Blaquiere, for $25,000, which left the syndicate with a small profit on the venture despite some $3750 in expenses for her voyage across the Atlantic and her campaign.

Commodore Stevens returned to America with the cup under his arm, and for the next six years it graced the mantel in his mansion on New York's Washington Square. But in 1857 the syndicate deeded the trophy as the America's Cup to the New York Yacht Club on the condition that it be held "perpetually a Challenge Cup for friendly competition between foreign countries."

Since then, twenty-one hard-fought contests have been staged for the "Auld Mug," as Sir Thomas Lipton, Bart., who himself mounted five famous challenges with his *Shamrocks* in the years from 1899 to 1930, dubbed it. This year's match race will be the twenty-second, and, as you all know, represents the fourth time Australia has entered the lists.

In those years the America's Cup has come to be regarded as the Golden Grail of yachting, not without some substance when you remember the uncounted millions of pounds, francs and dollars that have gone into challenges and defense, but the Americans have maintained an unbroken line of success. Even so, again as we all know, Australia has learned, and even now the historians are saying that our last effort in 1970 with *Gretel II* was the closest and most exciting in Cup history. And perhaps it was since *Gretel* actually won two of the five races, even though one of those wins was reversed at the protest table, still an unparalleled record.

This year, it is clearly apparent that Australia is going to Newport with the most finely thought-out, the most carefully prepared campaign we yet have mounted, and with a boat — as we look at her there in her slip — that gives us much confidence. It gives me great pride that the Royal Perth Yacht Club can count among its members a man of the sporting caliber of Alan Bond, and it gives me equally great pride to be commodore of the club delivering this challenge for that coveted trophy.

I am sure you all will join with me and with all the members of the Royal Perth Yacht Club in wishing Alan Bond, Godspeed, and every success in his endeavours.

— Adapted from the remarks of Commodore Alan Edwards on the occasion of the christening of *Southern Cross*, at Yanchep Sun City, Western Australia, Saturday, 12 January 1974, by Victor Jorgensen.

Contents

Foreword	vii
A Midas Touch	3
Young Man from Ealing	17
Joshua at the Gates	33
A Bear of a Genius	53
Wheels and Buttons	71
No Bludgers Here	85
Of Cloaks and Daggers	97
The Sound of Music	119
A Plate in the Floor	139
Still the Others	155

Hear our prayers O Lord,
And stretch out Your right hand
In blessing over this boat, the Southern Cross,
And to all who will sail in her,
Just as You granted your blessing to the Ark of Noah
Riding the waters of the flood.
Stretch out Your supporting hand, Lord,
As you stretched it out for Peter walking on the sea.
And send from Heaven, Your Holy Angel
To protect and keep safe from all dangers
This boat, the Southern Cross, and her crew.
Watch over Your sons who sail in her.
Keep them free from all adversity
And lead them home in safety from the seas they sail.
We pray that the efforts of all concerned
Be crowned with success.
We ask You this through Christ, our Lord.

Christening ceremony blessing
by the Reverend John O'Reilly.
Yanchep Sun City, Australia, 12 January, 1974.

" . . . this yacht will challenge on behalf of all of you."
Alan Bond told his guests.

12
KA4

A Midas Touch

THE CHRISTENING of an America's Cup yacht is a drama all its own. Will she or won't she float on her lines? Will she or won't she meet her designer's expectations? Will she or won't she be worth the millions lavished on her hull and campaign? For those who challenge for the America's Cup, christenings are pitched on a still higher emotional level because, coursing through the minds of every man involved, is the overweening question: Will she or won't she be the first challenger to break a 122-year winning streak – the longest in any sport?

The mid-summer sun shone hotly on the little crescent-shaped harbor at Yanchep Sun City. There, they say, the sun shines 365 days a year. The long white coastline of Australia stretching south to Perth glittered as it bathed in wind and water that had travelled unhindered across the Indian Ocean. Occasionally a wave struck the man-made mole, sending its cap spouting over the wall into the calm harbor beyond where the crayfish boats lay.

As homeport for Australia's fourth and latest challenger for the America's Cup, unlikely is not the word for Yanchep Sun City with its present population of some two thousand. Twenty-six miles north of Perth, the nearest city, some seventeen hundred and fifty miles southwest from Darwin, bordered by sea and desert, four hours by jet west of Sydney, Yanchep, whose aboriginal name comes from a species of bulrush, is a light year away from Newport, Rhode Island. Yet from this speck of a town, has come one of the most sophistically simple racing yachts ever seen anywhere — the first all-aluminum twelve-meter ever built. The incongruity is almost too great for the human intellect to grasp.

Held by the concrete fingers of her pen, the long, slim twelve-meter tugged at her mooring lines as if sensing the anomaly. Sandwiched between a wide white band along her sheer and her white bottom, the yellow hull cast wavy chartreuse patterns in the pale green water. They had labelled the yellow "mustard" but the irreverant crew had quickly come up with a better name. "Sun City yellow," they called it.

Customarily twelve-meters are painted white, or blue-green, or gray-blue, or maybe even maroon, or varnished. But yellow on white? Bright, strong and striking, here was something different.

But then everything about this unchristened challenger seemed different. Twelve-meter boats usually are christened and launched simultaneously, yet this nameless boat had been lowered surreptitiously into the water some weeks before at 7 o'clock in the evening at the edge of dark when no one was looking. Now she lay with her unique underbody demurely clad in Indian Ocean water, leaving only her topsides and rig exposed to the five hundred dignitaries crowding the marina's apron to witness the ceremony.

Dorothy Edwards, first lady of the recently elected Governor of Western Australia, was performing her maiden official rite as the wife of Air Commodore Hughie Edwards, V.C. With the morning seabreeze in her hair, she cut the ribbon holding the cunningly rigged champagne bottle. "I christen this ship *Southern Cross,*" she intoned. "May God keep safe all who sail in her."

The bottle clunked against the hull, and Mrs. Edwards wailed, "It didn't break."

"Have another go," shouted Alan Bond.

Mrs. Edwards tried again but the bottle bounced off intact.

"Very good glass," she remarked.

"You can see it's not too easy to win the Cup," Bond replied, "— or break the boat."

If she had been christened *La France,* the surprise couldn't have been greater. Although widely rumored that her name would undergo a last second change, for months the world and Australia had known the new challenger as *Australis.* Even the former Prime Minister William McMahon announced her name would be *Australis* at another ceremony way back in 1972, and surely he wouldn't deceive the public — particularly with an election in the offing.

Oh, other names had been kicked around. The inner circle, charged with making the decision, had toyed with Sundowner (too much like skidrow), Anzac, Shane, Acacia, Matilda (that smacked of the ill-starred defender *Dame Pattie*), and Waltzing Matilda. Then one night someone suggested Avenger. Avenger had a ring to it. A tough sound. It resounded with determination. It suggested the new boat would make amends for past losses. It was chosen.

The latest name was guarded with Manhattan Project-like security. No one breathed it and plaques were left blank until the last possible moment. But, as secrets will, this secret sprang a leak and with less than two days to go, someone spoiled the suspense by revealing that the new boat's name was *Avenger.*

So as a kilted pipe band and an honor guard from the Royal Australian Navy looked on, the burly crew stood at attention in their white-on-white sailing gear, and the crowd applauded as Mrs. Edwards let go with a muscle-twisting swing. The bottle shattered, spraying champagne over Australia's brightest challenger, *Southern Cross*.

It was among the first names that had been bandied about for the new challenger. It is one of the most popular boat names in Australia, gracing everything from dinks and tattered workboats, to freighters and dozens of yachts. But it also is the country's leitmotif, recognized in the farthest corner of the world, being borne on a field of blue in the nation's flag. The nation applauded.

By now the temperature had risen to mid-January heights and the honor guard of Royal Australian Navy men began to wilt and topple, so the guests adjourned to *Southern Cross'* cavernous shed where a feast and champagne by the bucketful bent the long tables. Nothing remained now for *Southern Cross* but to bring home to Australia the America's Cup.

Southern Cross amounts to an Everestian investment of time, manpower and money. From the outset, it was clearly spelled out that, whatever the cost, nothing but the best would go into the boat, the sails, crew, and the campaign. One man made that decision — Alan Bond. Although the syndicate also includes the aluminum firm, Comalco, which supplied the plate and some of the technology that went into the hull and spars as well as fifty thousand Australian dollars, and AMATIL of British Tobacco fame which contributed another $50,000, it was made clear at the beginning that Bond was boss. Unlike previous campaigns, no disrupting interference from other sponsors would be tolerated. Since *Southern Cross* cost more than $2,000,000 and the entire campaign more than $4,000,000, Bond had considerable clout for his no-nonsense attitude.

In terms of cash, what Bond bought was a boat that meets the Twelve-Meter Rule. That does not mean that she measures 39.37 feet but that after length, beam, girth, sail area, freeboard, and a lot of other arcane ingredients are entered in a formula and divided by 2.37, the answer must come up less than twelve meters or she doesn't qualify for the exclusive twelve-meter club.

If it sounds as though meeting these requirements would breed a fleet of look-alike twelve-meters, far from it. Even the untutored eye can pick out *Southern Cross,* for she is as different from any other twelve-meter as any America's Cup contender is from a Chinese sampan.

For those technically inclined and able to read into specifications and descriptions capabilities that may or may not be present in a boat, *Southern Cross* is a feast. To begin with, the only things she has in common with previous twelve-meters is that she sets a mainsail and jib, has a mast, a hull, winches, a keel, and is steered by a rudder. There resemblance parts.

There was little indication of this before the christening of *Southern Cross* although, as usual, rumors were abundant and extravagant. As an instance of how wide the credibility gap stretched, gossip in some of the sailing magazines had *Southern Cross* a shrimp with a mountain of sail. Predicted one correspondent "*Australis* (sic). gives the feeling that she is a small twelve . . . something which reinforces early rumors that Miller (designer Bob Miller) was planning a small yacht with lots of sail." Furthermore this misguided reporter had the temerity to suggest that *Southern Cross* resembled *Gretel II* — no one's candidate for prettiest boat of the era.

In any case, small *Southern Cross* is not. In fact she is one of the longer twelve meters. She measures sixty-seven feet from stem to stern which is three-and-a-half feet longer than *Intrepid,* the successful Cup defender in 1970, and *Gretel II* is a good five feet shorter than *Southern Cross* overall. *Southern Cross* displaces a lightweight 62,000 pounds. A comparison of beams has *Southern Cross* a hair-breadth narrower than *Gretel's* twelve feet six inches, but look alike? Tied up alongside each other in Yanchep marina, *Southern Cross* and *Gretel II* look as though they belong to different classes. A smallish mainsail is offset by a jib which spreads enough dacron to tent over the Yanchep Inn where the crews spent what off time they could scrape together before leaving for Newport and the main event.

But statistics tell little of shape. And shape, after all, is what separates one woman from another, a good boat from a bad one. In general, *Southern Cross* is a broad-shouldered, slim-hipped twelve-meter with a U-shaped entry and a simple deck layout. She accelerates rapidly, hobby-horses to a minimum, sails upwind as well as any optimist has the right to expect, and slides downwind like the wind itself.

Even a diletante receiving his first impression of *Southern Cross* senses her sheer purposefulness. As she heels into her work, her long overhangs fore and aft rapidly increase her waterline length so, as the old axiom goes, the product is nothing but speed. Moreover, after the relatively short-ended twelve-meters of previous campaigns, her appearance is a treat to behold, almost reminding one of racing craft of old — all tall spars, straight sheer, and long overhangs. A fast boat is a pretty boat and with her golden yellow hull tending to make her look still longer and lower, *Southern Cross* is on a par in beauty with her namesake, glittering high in the night sky.

The business end below the waterline is so radical that for weeks it was concealed from prying eyes. While travelling overland a special tube framework, draped with tarpaulins against the omnipresent cameras, confused the curious into thinking she had a bow such as American designer Britton Chance might draw. That was Miller's fine hand.

Had he been able to penetrate the screen, though, here is what a spy would have seen: In the 1970 fleet of twelve-meters, the leading edge from stem to the top of the ballast keel ran nearly straight or, at best, appeared slightly concave. Now look at the identical line on *Southern*

Cross. Like the others, she shows a knuckled bow — so sharp that during practice races off Yanchep an old section of tire was lashed to it as a fender for fear she would slice her trial horse in two — and a leading edge to keeltop that slopes away in a delicate hollow.

But now the similarity abruptly ends. For quite suddenly the line takes an astonishing dog-leg down into a big, well-shaped bosom, an appendage that looks quite unlike anything ever seen before on a twelve-meter, but ever so faintly reminiscent of the bulge at the bow of modern fast commercial and fighting ships. Miller's ocean racers are noted for broad shoulders around the mast but a chest like this is more than distinctive, it's unheard of.

What's it for? Before finally folding into her knife-edged ballast keel, the bosom soothes the bow wave into quiescence, or so the theory holds.

The ballast keel seems pedantic by comparison, yet isn't. It consists of a short, narrow, solid lead blade with identical sections running from top to shoe. Attached to a test model of *Gretel II* in the test tank, the blade increased her performance markedly. Unlike previous twelves, the keel carries no trim tab or flap on its trailing edge. Nevertheless the new blade seems to give *Southern Cross* plenty of lift and allows her to pirouette on her heel since the keel is short and placed far enough forward of the spade rudder to give her a rapid turning action. The ballast keel accounts for eighty percent or 55,000 pounds of *Southern Cross'* twenty-seven-and-a-half ton displacement.

Her expansive deck seems so flat and so clear that were it not for five cockpits, three coffee grinder drums, two self-tailing winches, a couple of spinnaker chutes up forward, the mast, and perhaps the skipper's hat, an airplane quite safely could alight on her deck. It's been said cockpits don't win America's Cup races but, it was felt, the efficient cockpit layout on *Southern Cross* couldn't hurt her either.

The aftermost cockpit contains twin large diameter steering wheels, the better to see to leeward and sight the genoa. (They learned the proper diameter from *Gretel II* whose tiny wheels gave the helmsmen endless arguments.) Next forward comes a triangular opening followed by a pair of smaller man-holes to port and starboard and, in turn, a trench just abaft the mast. These cockpits hold winch tailers, tactician, skipper, and navigator. Overall, though, the idea is to keep heads down and out of the wind. The spinnaker pole stows in its own sunken slot on the foredeck.

Nowadays the mainboom vang rides on a circular track mounted on the deck and *Southern Cross* is no exception. The only trouble was that to begin with the strains were so fierce that the deck began to lift when they vanged the boom down and extra supporting brackets had to be welded in down below. Otherwise, a theme of simplicity governs everything with no complicating fancy business allowed anywhere on deck. Down below, on the other hand, it's a different story.

In a close race with two boats tacking back and forth in a tacking duel, what goes on in the "engineroom" where the actual winching takes place can spell the difference between winning and losing. The search for winch power has even brought the suggestion that coffee grinder winches, those soul-crackers designed to trim jib and spinnaker gear, be peddled like bicycles rather than cranked by hand as they are today. But the standard grinder now still consists of a pedestal with a handle projecting from each side. These machines are mounted below decks in the racing machines where crewmen bend over them and wring out the wash.

Even though coffee grinders have improved with better gearing, more versatility and greater power, the perfect grinder is yet to be discovered, but Malcolm Barlow, Australia's premier winch maker, had added his bit for the new *Southern Cross* with a simplified and cleaner version of winches that first appeared aboard *Intrepid* in 1970. Instead of peddling or bending over their work, crankers on *Southern Cross* stand on specially designed platforms and wind what look like upside-down egg beaters. These winches are not mounted on deck but hang from the overhead. Barlow's winches are connected by a refined linkage system which allows the crankers to throw a lever and apply their muscle to selected winch drums.

The winch grinders below, too, easily can see the tailers hauling in the sheets just above them at their half-in half-out stations. This may seem unimportant aboard a wooden boat but, as they soon discovered aboard the first aluminum twelve-meter, the metal hull forms a colossal echo chamber and when wire sheets begin to drum the aluminum deck, communications became all but impossible. If a tailer jams his sheet and yells "round turn!" the grinders below might not hear his cries for years. A small item, perhaps, but possibly crucial in a tacking duel.

For the rest of it, the crew below sees nothing but sky, hears nothing but bedlam. All orders during maneuvers either come by signal or instinct. One crewman, working deep in the bowels of *Southern Cross,* became completely disoriented during an early practice session.

"We're so deep in the boat," he complained, "that we couldn't tell what the hell was happening. We didn't know whether the boat was tacking, jibing, running, reaching, or hard on the wind."

The skipper soon straightened out his puzzled crew. Helpfully, he told them he'd been sailing in circles.

As for orders, the skipper need only whisper his commands into the cockpit for them to resound throughout the hull like the product of some giant bullhorn. And at the helm, skipper John Cuneo, as we shall discover, is not accustomed to whispering. Still, by starting months before any of their rivals, the crew enjoyed an advantage because they could accustom themselves to the rattle and bang of sailing an aluminum twelve-meter—a lesson no one had learned before.

Soaring aloof over the drumming racket below stands a ninety-foot mast, the longest extrusion ever produced in Australia by syndicate member Comalco. Bedecking the mast is a deck-sweeping boom and a tracery of running and standing rigging that looks completely foreign to previous rather clumsy affairs on Australian challengers. The mast is beautifully shaped, bends smoothly to its controls and, indeed, evokes visions of the lightweight, finely thought-out rigs of the defenders.

Some of the sails in *Southern Cross'* sail locker came from designer Miller's own loft; many mains and genoas from Peter Cole's Australian Hood loft. North Sails of Australia provided others while Rolly Tasker, who owns lofts all over the world but first and foremost is an Australian, supplied the rest.

Whatever her destiny, to watch *Southern Cross* under way is to witness power and symmetry in motion. The extraordinary thing about her is that, thanks to her unusual lines, she slides through the water with no fuss. Bill Lucas, who sailed trial horse *Gretel II* against her in the early tilts, said the most astonishing thing to him was that *Southern Cross* always seemed motionless until suddenly he would realize she was drawing farther and farther away. A huge yellow ghost, she would sail away leaving no notice of her coming, no notice of her going. Already she has built that mystique without which no boat is a winner.

It is hard to escape the feeling that should her challenge for the America's Cup come adrift or even should she lose in the challenge selection trials that . . . well . . . it won't be her fault.

Even designer Miller, who once claimed he would rather design a steam roller than a twelve-meter, was surprised by her first demonstration. Until he actually saw her sail, Miller had warned owner Alan Bond that

Australia didn't hold a prayer of capturing the Cup. Then he saw *Southern Cross* under way and suddenly, said Miller afterwards, "I began to believe Australia's chances were good."

However, when all is said and done, a boat is a boat and hope, a gust of wind. People design boats. People build them. People cut their sails. And other people crew. A man, a mere mortal with all of man's frailties, steers *Southern Cross*. Furthermore, someone else again orchestrates men and machine and unless the entire combination hums . . . phut! . . . the man who pays the bills takes a bath.

With this in mind, the *Southern Cross* campaign is probably the most daring challenge in the long history of the America's Cup. And it all began with a young sign painter from Ealing, Alan "Bondy" Bond.

Bond concentrates on the helm.

Alan Bond waits as Mrs. Edwards launches the champagne bottle, one, two three times before spattering Southern Cross *for good luck.*

The Southern Cross *and proud owner.*

12

KA4

Young Man from Ealing

Bounding off the steamer *Himalaya,* thirteen-year-old emigre Alan Bond greeted his new country with both excitement and trepidation. The ship's tall flanks loomed above him and the aroma of steam and oil mingled sharply with the smell of dock water flowing out of the Swan River at Fremantle. Bond had arrived in his new home in Australia and for those very first moments, it felt very alien to him. He had left England with a cold, blowing winter in the air. Now his world stood upside down, and suddenly it was mid-summer in January.

At that time in 1950, Bond couldn't afford a kayak, so there was little reason for him to guess that twenty-three years later, almost to the month, his own twelve-meter yacht would be offloaded from Sydney at the same dock. Rags to riches, the Midas touch, tycoon, luck — all are clichés to Bond. He won his fortune by hard work, quick thinking, stubborness, and the fun of overcoming challenges.

Bond still recalls his early days in Fremantle vividly and with cheerfulness.

"Most kids have more or less decided something by the time they reach thirteen, but I had decided nothing," he said years later. "Coming to a new country, things are always harder the first couple of years because everything is so strange. I didn't know anyone. Everyone was set in their ways. They were going to school and all had their families. They had grown up together."

It was a difficult adjustment for Bond in the beginning, but he made it and began to shoot down new roots in his adopted soil. Bond's native roots in England had been severed when the family left Britain. And had it not been for war injuries suffered by his father Frank, a Royal Air Force veteran, Bond still probably would be planted in London near his birthplace at Ealing. And unless he had been an immigrant who became a self-made Australian multi-millionaire, it also is probable that he would not now be challenging for the America's Cup under the aegis of the Royal Perth Yacht Club.

Actually, Bond can thank his father's doctors for the fact he became a larger-than-life Australian. His father had been told by English doctors that if he continued to live in England's dreary climate, he would die within two years. On the other hand, if he moved to Australia they might give him an additional eight years. Confronted with that ultimatum, the Bond family had no choice but to pick up and move to Perth's better climate half a world away. There Frank Bond thrived and fooled everyone, including the doctors, by living not only the ten years maximum the doctors gave him, but another eleven years on top of it. Frank Bond died in 1971.

Happy though the early outcome was, the move from England nevertheless had its bit of trauma for the Bonds as one senses from the poignant comment Bond's mother once made to a friend. "Once our house in England was sold, there was no going home again," she had said.

With his mother, father, and older sister, Bond settled into a small East Fremantle apartment and was shipped off to Fremantle Boys School. But outgoing, inquisitive Bond, who swarms with ideas and seethes at rote, quickly discovered he needed Fremantle Boys the way Fremantle Boys needed him. Besides, money was hard to come by. So despite his age, he quit school at fourteen and enrolled in night classes where his subjects included accounting, English, tinsmithing, woodworking, and art or "finger painting," as Bond now calls it. He had in mind the building trade. That took care of his evenings.

His days were filled by splashing paint on storefronts, tall chimneys and posters for hamburger stands as a fifty-dollar-a-month apprentice sign painter. Maintaining his jet-propelled pace, he married Eileen Theresa Hughes at 17 and settled down to becoming a family man. One of Bond's great gifts has been his ability to instantly size up people and in vivacious Eileen Theresa, his gifts once more proved infallible. What Eileen saw in Bond was a 5′7″ bundle of energy, a round, tough winner. The Bond family now comprises two sons and two daughters.

Two years later, Bond came to the conclusion — some say brashly — that he had the organizational ability to run a fifty-man painting operation better than the next man, so he floated a company called Nu-Signs. Nu-Signs specialized in jobs other companies wouldn't touch. It prospered. It also dealt in renovating decrepit houses which Bond would rebuild and sell at a profit despite pessimists who said the buildings were too far gone to fix.

Bond responds to pessimism the way the Australian bush responds to a match. For example, when everyone claimed the hills beyond Perth were too steep for development, the 21-year-old Bond reacted by borrowing $200,000 from a company that he had persuaded to enter the land mortgage business in Western Australia. Then, slicing into those hills, he built roads and drafted the plan of a subdivision called Lesmurdie Heights and another named Sunset Ridge. The lots sold as fast as he carved them out until, to the amazement of his creditors, every penny of the $200,000 was repaid within six weeks. Suddenly, Bond of Nu-Signs became Bond the land developer; credit rating A-1.

Coup followed coup in staccato succession, including his recent foray into Robe River. Robe River lies over eight hundred miles north of Perth on the edge of the Great Sandy Desert and is considered by many to be the richest iron ore deposit in the world with a value of something over a billion Australian dollars. The area also holds other minerals, oil, and natural gas. Just last year, an opportunity cropped up for Bond to invest in Robe River and, as the stunned financial community watched, he siezed control of $97 million worth of stock with a $1.7 million deposit on what were called the longest, tidiest terms in history. The deal bears Bond's meticulously carved stamp all over it.

Still, Bond maintains Yanchep Sun City, where the sun shines ceaselessly, represents his real triumph. "They" predicted he couldn't build Sun City either, yet there it stands. Sun City covers 20,000 rolling acres of virgin sand and scrub fronting on the Indian Ocean. Bond wangled the rights to the beach from the government which until then had refused to give up so much as an inch, let alone the eleven miles Bond wanted. As skeptics continued to tell him he was long out of his mind, Bond laid roads, marked out lots, erected a town center, watched as houses shot up daily, and built the first of three golf courses. In time, Bond sees Sun City as a billion-dollar development inhabited by 200,000 people from Perth, Sydney, Melbourne, New York, London — people searching for the sound of sea and wind rather than the screech of brakes and the honk of horns.

On the shore below Sun City lies the Yanchep marina where *Southern Cross* was launched and where she lay before leaving for the United States. It will become one of three man-made harbors for the use of crayfishermen and pleasure boats but in the early months of 1974, it belonged to Bond's twelve-meters. And no twelve-meter ever enjoyed a base camp like *Southern Cross'*. An echoing, windowless shed hid *Southern Cross* when she left the water. The shed also contained a carpeted locker room for the crews, an office for the skipper, another for designer Bob Miller, and a kitchen. Under the same roof was a complete workshop, showers, and a fully equipped sail loft with sewing machines and a horizontal mast for checking sails. To haul *Southern Cross* out of the water and into her cocoon, Bond imported a huge travel-lift, the only one of its kind in Australia. Overlording the establishment was a guard to keep out spies during the day while at night a Doberman Pinscher, who even scared Bond, went on duty.

In the previous three Australian challenges, the boats were based at Sydney where it took hours to tow out of the harbor and through the Heads to the open ocean for practice. As a consequence, they could squeeze in only a few practice races each day and on water that little resembled the conditions off Newport, with generally heavier winds and larger seas. At Yanchep, the practice course lay five minutes sailing time from dock to a piece of ocean whose water closely matched Newport, particularly early and late in the day when the onshore and offshore breezes filled in.

But above all, the sensation of standing on the "wailing wall" — a huge, hand-laid stone retaining wall behind the shed — and staring down at three twelve-meters — *Southern Cross* and both *Gretels* — moored so far away from Newport seemed as real as Alan Bond. They said he couldn't build Sun City, yet there it was. They say he can't win the America's Cup, either.

As Executive Director of the Bond Corporation, Bond operates from the seventeenth floor of one of Perth's newest, shiniest buildings. One softly enters his opulent office in the Bond organization's own International House through huge stainless steel doors which open onto a carpet whose pile feels only slightly thicker than looks the pile on the carpet which lines the ceiling. Buttons and switches operate the lights and curtains which sometimes conceal a stunning view of the Swan River flowing just a block away.

Outside his office in the dimly lit foyer near the elevator bank hangs a directory board listing twenty-nine Bond-controlled companies. In a way, they profile the man himself. It starts with the Bond Corporation Pty. Ltd., and runs through such varied enterprises as Eveready Finance Co. Pty. Ltd., the Steamship Building Pty. Ltd., the Yanchep Estates, before winding to an end with Tranby Estates Pty. Ltd. As an instance of how far afield Bond's enterprises range and how they proliferate, he once bought into a steamship line and right away used his newly acquired vessels to ship sheep he purchased to the Middle East. Bond leaves few stones unturned.

He stresses youth in his executive corps. That youngster in the modish shirt may be an office boy, then again he may be a senior executive. That young man in the elevator might be a salesman, but more than likely he is a director of the Bond Corporation. As of 1974, only one man on the Board is over forty and some haven't hit thirty. The 37-year-old Bond needs youth because he expects his executives to work night and day tirelessly, and if necessary, weekends, too. Bond believes in delegating authority but once delegated, the work had better be done . . . and done fast.

He reciprocates, however, with spontaneous generosity. One employee's wife in Perth could not overcome her homesickness for England, so Bond quietly sent her back to England for as long as she liked — all expenses paid. Another man was driving last year's Rover. "Don't you think you need a new one?" asked Bond, offering to buy him this year's model. "Well . . .", hesitated the man, and when next seen he was behind the wheel of a bright new Mercedes.

Perfect, though, Bond isn't. He has made land deals that have fallen flat, and he has said things he regrets. He owns a pair of Rolls Royces and his wife Eileen tools around Perth and Yanchep in the Cornische. Bond himself took up sports cars for a time but survived that experience only to nearly lose it all when he turned to big American autos. While driving down the road one day, he met a huge animal head on — wrecking his bright red Chevy.

"What'd you hit, a cow?" asked someone afterwards.

"No," laughed Bond with a roar, "a bull."

Bond quite understandably has a strong affection for Western Australia. Not alone because he rode the western land boom to a fortune, but because the country adopted him without prejudice. Those roots that were so important to him in 1950 no longer are tentative but grip fast to Western Australia.

"No one ever heard of Perth or Western Australia," Bond once snorted characteristically, "until all the lights were turned on when Colonel Glenn flew over in his space capsule. Now we've challenged for the America's Cup and people are going to realize not only that we're here, but what we've got!"

By what we've got, he means Australia.

The Bond family lives in a huge house on the Swan River which winds down through Perth from Darling Scarp, the ragged edge that marks the uplands holding Western Australia's lonely deserts. The house contains a fine collection of Seventeenth and Eighteenth Century art collected by art lover and finger painter Bond on his endless world travels. He especially cherishes an etching of Christ by Rembrandt. Fringing the river front is a swimming pool that some facetiously have claimed is large enough to hold the 635,000 population of Perth. But Bond, an excellent swimmer who still staunchly supports the life-saving club he once belonged to, insists his family maintain the Bond swimming tradition. Although reputedly unathletic, Bond also once played a pretty fair 5/8ths at Rugby and he waterskis zealously on occasion.

That is when he is not performing his elected but voluntary duties as a Councillor of the City of Perth.

But with all that, he still heads, on vacations and days off, for the brick chalet at Yanchep which overlooks the Indian Ocean and the endless dazzling beach. On those days the chalet is in constant motion with Bonds, pets, and friends.

Ask Bond how he got into sailing and the answer is straightforward yet notably preposterous. According to Bond, he owned a couple of farms in the country which a man wanted to buy but, unfortunately, lacked the down payment. Bond had been working extremely long hours at the time and was sitting in his office thinking he needed to get into some kind of sport to relax when the potential farm buyer called up. He wanted to know if Bond would accept a boat in place of cash for the down payment. A few minutes later, Bond owned a boat.

The sloop Bond accepted might have awed a seasoned sailor but in his ignorance, Bond didn't blink an eye. Forty-nine feet long, *Panamuna* had the deserved reputation in Western Australia of being a low-slung, overrigged, very, very fast weapon and, like a loaded gun, wasn't to be fooled with. Bond knew none of this when he drove down to the Royal Perth Yacht Club for the first sail. There *Panamuna's* regular crew eagerly awaited the new owner. To test him, they planned to start him off with the most unfathomable piece of gear aboard — the steering wheel.

"Okay, so there's the wheel," Bond said later. "I'd never been on a boat before so they hand me the wheel! It was a disaster."

About the only mistake he didn't make was to sink *Panamuna,* and in two months he blew two masts out of his forty-nine-foot down-payment because in his characteristically overpowering way, he carried too much sail in too much wind in his hurry to get there . . . anywhere.

Bond, despite endless bouts with seasickness, came to love sailing. Today he wryly recalls when he first took up sailing he would stand at the wheel feeling so weak from chucking over the side that he didn't think he could survive, and occasionally his seasickness got to the point where he truly hoped he wouldn't. Crewmen report his head would wobble so they dared not look at him. But he stuck it out, and eventually conquered seasickness altogether.

Since *Panamuna* he has raced in some of the world's most cruel and torturing contests. He has under his belt two and a half Sydney-Hobart races — the half representing the time the rudder fell off one of his boats. His ocean racing log includes two Fastnets, two Bermuda races, thirty races across the English Channel, other European events and, finally, one Transatlantic from Bermuda to Spain. It is a record that well might make Ahab's stomach churn.

As with most everything that has happened to Bond, there had been few portents of coming events back on that day he disembarked from the *Himalaya,* but certainly the one that would have been farthest from mind then was a meeting that took place early this last March when Yanchep received a royal visitor. On that day, the lad from Ealing found himself conducting His Royal Highness, Prince Philip of England, on a spin in the new twelve-meter. For three hours the Sailor Prince savored the rattle and bang of a match race, and then, expert helmsman that he is, took the wheel himself and pronounced *Southern Cross* a right royal piece of equipment. Bond, for once just a little awed, beamed.

A different side of Bond's extroverted personality emerges when he talks ocean racing — a sensitive, introspective side.

"I get a tremendous feeling from sailing at night," he told me. "The sun goes down and the stars are never as bright as they are on the ocean. Only people who have been ocean racing would believe it. And the stillness.

"The sun sets on the boat, and there you are. It's always beautiful. And in the morning when the sun rises, the air has a freshness all its own. It's quite different from anything you will experience anywhere except on the sea."

There are men who have faced Bond across a conference table who no doubt wish they had met him at sea. Vic Romagna, who crewed on the unsuccessful American Cup contender *Valiant* in 1970, may come to join that coterie. Officially Bond's reason for challeging for the America's Cup is to represent Australia with the strongest, best prepared challenger in history. It also may be to put vast but thinly populated Western Australia on the map by using Sir Thomas Lipton's famous tactics for selling tea. But there is a personal score to settle, too.

Indeed, if *Southern Cross* does happen to capture the America's Cup, the New York Yacht Club need not mount the defending skipper's head in place of the Cup in the Cup's glass case, as has been suggested so often. Instead, they might try Vic Romagna's silvery head for size. Because it was none other than Romagna that started Bond as the youngest challenger for the world's greatest yachting prize.

Prince Philip, the Duke of Edinburgh, enjoys a joke with Alan Bond, Jim Hardy and the crew.

Broad reach and flying fast, the Prince takes the helm of Southern Cross.

Avid yachtsman, Sir Charles Gardener, ex-Governor of Western Australia, chats with Alan Bond.

Alan and Eileen Bond pose with Doug Anthony, former Deputy Prime Minister of Australia.

Air Commodore Hughie Edwards meets skipper John Cuneo.

The hope of Australia, Southern Cross.

12

KA4

Joshua at the Gates

ONLY MAN'S MAKER can truly fathom what drives anyone to try for the America's Cup. Some have said fame. Some have said sheer cussedness. Some have said the challenge itself. Sir Frank Packer, in one of his garrulous moments, blamed "alcohol and delusions of grandeur." But what really impels rich men to spend mountains of money on a sport that until now has led nowhere but to defeat and to astronomical bills, is difficult to understand. Yet the longer the winning streak, the greater the urge to break it . . . at whatever price.

Lord Dunraven tried to win the Cup twice in 1893 and 1895, but became so infuriated on losing that he laid about with rancorous and intemperate charges which brought him nothing other than being drummed from his honorary membership in the New York Yacht Club. He gave up, a disheartened and puzzled old man.

Sir Thomas Lipton at first was looked down upon as nothing more than an Irish peddler who had challenged with his *Shamrock* to sell tea. But he, too, came down with Cup fever and by the time he lost the fifth contest in his 31-year campaign at the age of eighty-two, his loyal public no longer called his obsession the America's Cup Races, but the Lipton Races. No longer was it Sir

Thomas, the showman, but Sir Thomas, the sportsman. The America's Cup breaks, and the America's Cup makes.

Following World War II, the twelve-meters arrived and with them came men of Baron Bich and Sir Frank Packer's cut. Baron Marcel Bich of France undoubtedly sold a gross or two of the ballpoint pens for which he is so famous when he tackled the Australians for the right to challenge for the Cup in 1970. But, like his predecessors, Cup fever soon overcame whatever disappointment he may have suffered and he entered the lists again for 1974 with nothing on his mind but taking the unreachable Cup home to France.

News magnate Sir Frank Packer similarly may have peddled a newspaper for every dollar he spent on his first *Gretel,* but was it newspapers or the Cup that drove him back to Newport in 1970 with *Gretel II*?

Alan Bond has his own feelings on the subject of challenging and he has expressed them on more than one occasion unabashedly.

"Anyone who considers that racing for the Cup isn't a business proposition is a bloody fool," he once told a reporter. "There can be no justification for spending six million dollars on the Australian challenge unless the return is going to involve more than just an ornate silver pitcher."

Inevitably, though, and despite the fact he never lost sight of the Cup's value to Sun City, Alan Bond quickly succumbed to the same fever as his precursors. And he has no one to blame for planting the first germ other than Vic Romagna.

Vic Romagna is a tolerable man. His neighbors like him. He doesn't beat dogs. He has crewed on more America's Cup contenders and defenders than anyone, and he is always in demand as a shipmate on crack ocean racers. If he has a fault, it is loyalty, which explains what happened when he was working aboard *Valiant* one day in Bob Derecktor's yard at Mamaroneck, New York. As a crewman aboard the Cup defense contender, he spotted a big foreign bloke peering nosily into *Valiant's* cockpit, and Romagna saw red.

The face belonged to Bob Miller who designed Alan Bond's *Apollo* – *Panamuna's* replacement – which lay nearby being readied for a Bermuda Race. Much of *Apollo's* gear had been stowed in the same shed as *Valiant's*. As a goodwill gesture to their neighbors, the Australians had wrapped a case of beer in an Australian flag for *Valiant's* crew.

"Hey!" shouted Romagna, thinking Miller was soaking up *Valiant's* secrets, "bugger off." (These are Miller's words.) As he remembers it, Romagna added a couple more uncomplimentary details before chiding, "If you were home watching TV and some bloke came along and stuck his face in your window, you'd tell him to piss off, too."

"Listen, mate," retorted the king-sized Miller, "we're not interested in your bloody boat or Cup. If we were, we'd come back and win it all off yer."

At that point it looked as though the *Apollo* and *Valiant* men might square off on Derecktor's pier in a small-scale riot. Bond, though, remembered the beer. Anyone who acted like "Romango," as he still calls Romagna, didn't deserve to wet his lips on good Australian suds. He yelled to one of his crew to retrieve the case before it fell into Yankee hands. With that, somewhat unaccountably, the tension eased and peace returned.

But it was at that moment that Bond began to think, "Well, why not?"

Still thinking "Why not?" Bond returned from his ocean racing sorties to Bermuda and Europe mulling the details of the project. Bond works like that. He makes a snap decision on some one, some thing, then analyzes his decision to the last shred. By September of 1970, he felt ready and cabled the New York Yacht Club to inform them he would like to challenge for the elusive prize. A cable from the Royal Perth Yacht Club was received later, making the challenge official in New York.

With Bond's energetic reputation in mind, his request created a stir not only in the New York Yacht Club but outside the club as well. It also created some anxiety over the thought of perhaps sailing the matches at Yanchep, if he won. For example, while dining at Newport's Clambake Club one night with the New York Yacht Club's paterfamilias, Henry Morgan, Bond was asked by Mrs. Morgan, "If you win the Cup, you will sail it off Newport, won't you?"

To which Bond gallantly replied, "Well, we'll have to have a look into this, won't we? Maybe we can have one every two years: one match off Yanchep and the other off Newport." It was Joshua at the gates.

Challenging for the apparently unbudgeable Cup is more than a matter of sending a single cable, though, because other challengers invariably demand to get into the act. In 1974 — apart from the Royal Perth — the French, the Canadians, and the Royal Thames Yacht Club of Great Britain also had challenged. As a matter of fact, it was the Royal Thames challenge that the New York Yacht Club formally accepted.

But it was accepted with limitations since the New York club had grown tired of the problems created by multiple challenges which placed the club in a position not unlike the lady of the night, besieged by suitors, deciding upon whom she would bestow her favors. The solution was simple and widely acclaimed in the sailing world when the club ruled for the 1970 challenges that it would send its selected defender against whichever challenger succeeded in winning a series of trials conducted by the nominal challenging club off Newport. That established a series of trials much like the series held for years by the multiple American contenders for the honor of defending the cup. It also partly removed one of the hoary excuses for losing that pointed out the challenger never had the benefit of blood bath competition before she met the defender.

In 1970, as the record book shows, Australia's *Gretel II* bested France's *France* in four straight matches in the first challenger eliminations, but, at this writing, just who will be contending for the 1974 challenge — and, for that matter, who will be contending for the defense — is about as firm as the proverbial bowl of jelly.

The Canadians have long since withdrawn; the French, who originally announced a new boat, have decided to try again with the first *France;* the English are on-again, off-again, but whatever the outcome will conduct the challenger trials. In that sea of vacillation, though, there has been not the slightest question about Australia's effort. Alan Bond and his *Southern Cross* will be there — barring some cataclysm that would have to be cataclysmic, indeed.

Bond is no starry-eyed Quixote when it comes to tackling anyone, and the Americans in particular. Without having challenged before, he doesn't really believe any country can win the Cup.

"I don't think any country can expect to win the first time out," he has said. "Winning depends on a build-up of knowledge, handed down from one challenge to the other, and looking and analyzing why a boat failed to win the series. That's what gives you a better situation."

One of the greatest criticisms Bond levels at the challenge system is that the New York Yacht Club is under no obligation to offer a challenging club a return match if it loses the first time.

"The reason they don't do that is the more you try against them, the better your chances of beating them become until finally you win," he contends. "When the club says, 'Well, we want to give another country an opportunity,' I don't think they are altogether following the best interests of yachting and I don't think it's in the best interests of the Cup itself."

It is the continuity of knowledge gathered from defense to defense that has given the defender the edge, and nothing more, Bond feels. With *Southern Cross,* he means to break that continuity and start a streak of his own.

Nor is Bond quixotic about his boat's chances in 1974. Deep down he believes *Southern Cross* will win, yet taking into account the populations of Australia versus the United States, the number of unsuccessful challenges, the number of races won by challengers in 123 years, and the number of races won by Australian challengers, he gives odds of ten to one. That is, he guesses *Southern Cross* has one chance in ten of winning against the Americans.

Is the America's Cup a sporting contest or a blood sport? In Bond's view, it is a sporting contest. But it is also more than that. It is a fight to the finish with no room for mistakes.

"Once you get knocked down, you are finished in this kind of racing. I just have to hope we have that bit more will-to-win," he said just before leaving Australia for Newport.

In preparing for combat, Bond examined the reasons for past Australian failures microscopically. Principally, he learned what often seems obvious but isn't: that campaigns usually get under way too late. *Gretel II's* campaign started up so late that, before she met *Intrepid,* she had sailed only four matches in anger and those were against her rival challenger *France.* Meanwhile, *Intrepid* had sailed thirty-three knuckle-down contests in winning her right to defend. Until her arrival in Newport ten days before she met *France, Gretel II* had not so much as set a staysail, yet she was the Royal Sydney Yacht Squadron's hope.

Well warned, *Southern Cross* hit the water months ahead of her foreign rivals and by September, 1974, her picked crew was well versed in match racing combat, having undergone over a year's worth of no-holds-barred clashes between the *Gretels* and *Southern Cross*. That, Bond said, should develop the required jugular instinct.

Bond also acquired another significant lesson from the previous Australian campaigns. He learned that *Gretel II* had been plagued by crew confusion right through the ultimate matches against *Intrepid* because the final crew had been picked almost at the last minute from two different trial crews. Even during the main feature, they were trying to mold themselves into a single team. Bond was told that skipper Jim Hardy, accompanied by two other would-be skippers in the cockpit, found himself not only trying to maintain his own role as skipper, but also had his hands full organizing the entire campaign — too much responsibility was left in his hands. "There were too many chiefs, not enough Indians," Hardy agrees. It also was too much of a load for one man, particularly the skipper.

There would be no friction, no overloading aboard *Southern Cross*. On *Southern Cross* everything was spelled out before the first weld went into her aluminum hull. The skipper would command, the crew would crew, and everyone would learn to do nothing but his best. There would be no confusion about who did what, when, or how. Bond saw to that.

Apparently, it has worked as designed, because one crewman, who had sailed aboard *Gretel II,* reported: "I can't get over the difference. Last time you had to get people off their butts to do anything. This time if anything needs doing, when you come ashore it is done right now." Said another, "There's an atmosphere of professionalism around here."

Alan Bond learned to in-fight, too. When it was announced that Danish sailor Paul Elvstrom, the world's most gifted sailor, would be Baron Bich's skipper on *France* along with an all-Scandinavian crew, Bond quietly went to work in the right quarters. He suggested it would be highly inappropriate for a Dane to be sailing a French boat against *Southern Cross* and he took an even dimmer view of some experiments for the French effort that were conducted in a Scandinavian test tank. After all, there has been a long-standing requisite that a Cup challenger — or defender, for that matter — be a product solely of the country of her origin. Bond's entire stand was made unofficially, and whether his complaint had any effect or not is, perhaps, moot but, as 1973 waned, Elvstrom and crew were off the French boat and Bich had decided against building a new boat at all. Instead, he would enter the lists with his defeated but re-vamped *France I*.

Chiefly, though, Bond learned that he needed a czar to oversee the entire operation. Not a dictator, but a boss capable of coping with every problem from finding a bunk for a visiting fireman to locating the right size block for a *Southern Cross* replacement. Without such a conductor to orchestrate the operation, confusion could run wild and, again, the campaign could end in another loss. As we shall discover, in syndicate manager Brian Leary, Bond found such a boss.

But well oiled though the *Southern Cross* operation seemed, it has met its share of resistance in the homeland. To Australians, an America's Cup challenge is more than a duel between one club and another, one boat and another. Like the Davis Cup in tennis, it is a sporting duel "between them and us," and Australians are known the world over for their concern with such duels.

It is, perhaps, not entirely surprising that in view of that concern, gloom-and-doomers were even more vociferous than the staunch supporters. In any case, while *Southern Cross* was readying herself for the contest, the gloomers were heard from Sydney to Perth, from Brisbane to Darwin. They had heard it all before, they moaned. There had been bickering amongst syndicate members before, and there would be bickering again.

There had been predictions of great victories over the Yanks and the predictions had turned to ash. They would again.

The new boat, they glumly pointed out, was owned by a sailing novice, designed by an eccentric who never had designed a twelve-meter before, manned by a green crew which never had sailed together previously and, most significantly of all, was skippered by a man who never had sailed in big boat match races until 1973, and one who never had skippered a twelve-meter. They foresaw nothing other than another bitter batch of second-guessing and recriminations on losing.

But not Bond. Sir Thomas Lipton may have earned his stripes as "the world's best loser." That doesn't interest Bond. He doesn't know the meaning of the word. Despite his odds estimate, losing to Bond is simply bad manners, and he has inculcated his *Southern Cross* team with the same outlook.

Since winning is both warp and woof of his master plan, Alan Bond ignored some skilled veterans of previous campaigns because they had been cogs in machines that broke down. He wanted nothing to do with losers, whatever their qualifications. Even though designer Alan Payne created *Gretel I* and the ugly but swift *Gretel II* and is Australia's foremost naval architect, Bond wanted no part of him. Whether it was his fault or not, Payne had been associated with a pair of twelve-meters that lost, and therefore Bond struck Payne's name from the list.

The same applied to Warwick Hood. Hood was the only other naval architect in sparsely populated Australia with twelve-meter qualifications and experience, but he had designed *Dame Pattie* which lost to *Intrepid* four, love.

Scratch Hood, too. Clearly what Bond needed was someone fresh, someone different — a winner. The man Bond needed, he decided, was an unknown musical quiz-kid named Bob Miller.

Man-made Yanchep Marina on the dazzling Indian Ocean.

Yanchep Sun City under construction with the marina beyond where future Cup races may be held.

It took sixteen weeks and $200,000 to build this hanger to service Southern Cross *at Yanchep.*

Ex-challenger Gretel II *arrives intact to work as trial horse with* Southern Cross.

Decked out in camouflage, Southern Cross *arrives at Fremantle from her builders in Sydney,*

— and is trucked thirty miles north to Yanchep for her launching in the Indian Ocean.

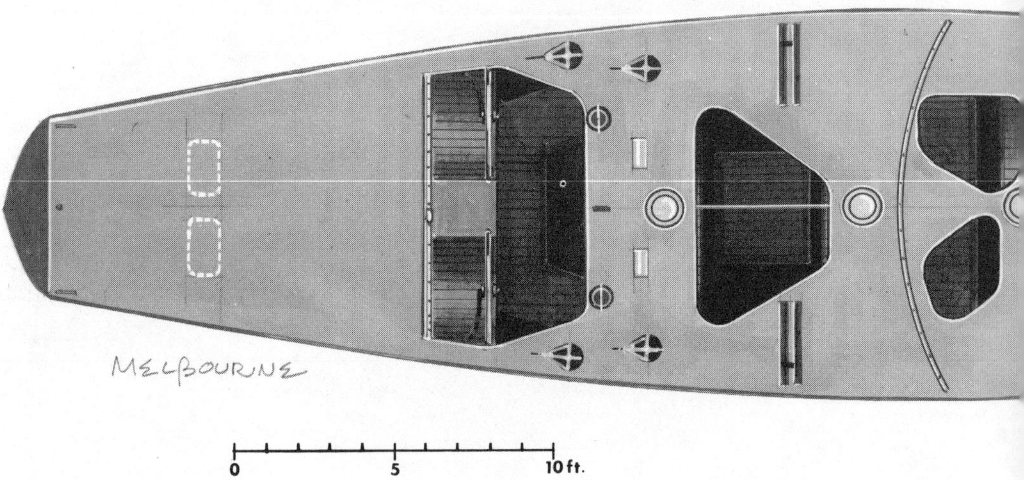
MELBOURNE
0
5
10 ft.

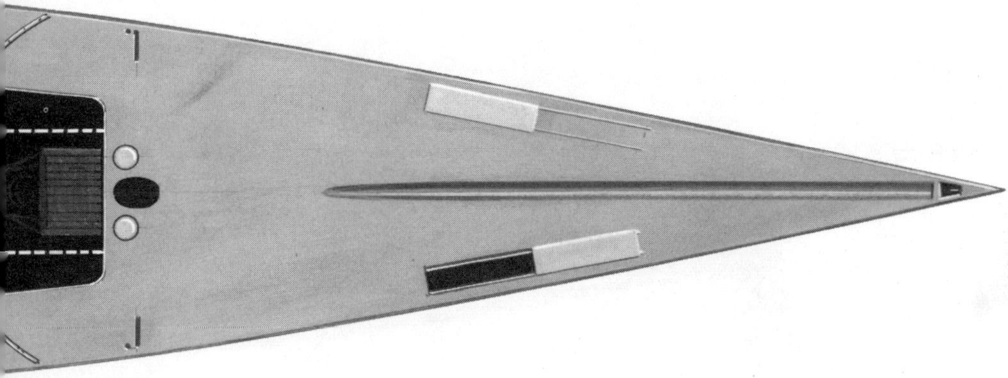

Deck view of Southern Cross *reveals cockpits and odd-shaped deck openings. Dotted lines indicate changes undertaken prior to departure from Australia. Foredeck hatches launch spinnakers, and circular tracks control boom vangs.*

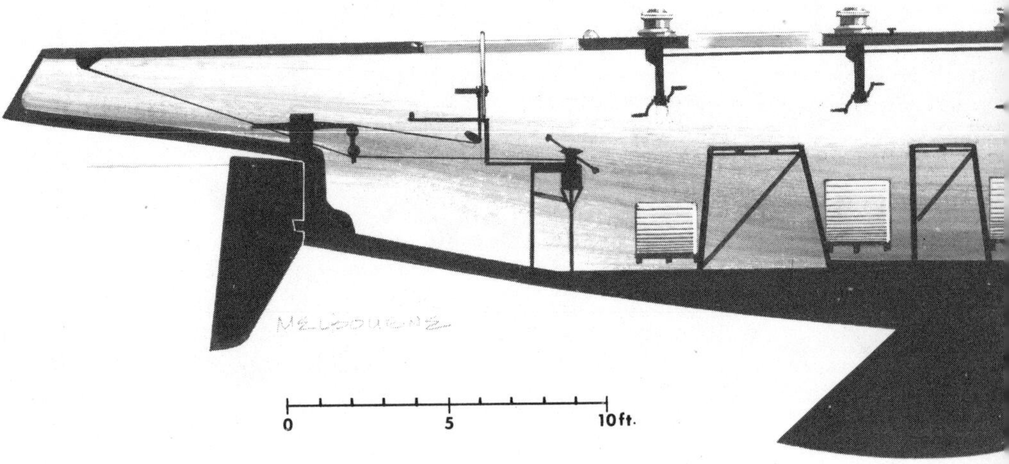
0
5
10ft.

Cutaway profile of Southern Cross *designed by Bob Miller reveals short keel, deep rudder, and bosomed underbody. The main winches are linked amidships and the winches for backstays and halyards are below decks.*

Bob Miller with model of Apollo, *the first ocean racer he designed for Alan Bond.*

12

KA4

A Bear of a Genius

WERE IT NOT FOR Robert Miller's parents, Alan Bond would have needed to have Miller built. Bob Miller is a big, bearish, eclectic who speaks so quietly that his voice comes across on a tape recorder as nothing louder than a dim murmur. Miller's singular slant on life, his utter independence, and his driving need to design distinctive, winning boats put him right in Bond's camp from the beginning.

Striking in appearance from stem to stern, Miller's boats are as unusual as he is himself. So the story goes, when Bond telephoned Miller to order a replacement for *Panamuna,* Miller hung up on him as a sailing inch-brow. But Bond's stubborn streak matches Miller's and Bond persisted until Miller finally accepted his call. Although hard up and still buried in the shadow of Alan Payne and Warwick Hood, Miller is supposed to have said:

"Okay, I'll design you a boat but I'll tell you how long she's going to be, how wide, what she'll draw, how she'll look, and while she's building you won't interfere. All you will do is pay the bill."

With that, Miller slapped Bond with an estimate that was calculated to make even a self-made millionaire's ears ring. Nonetheless, Bond ordered his first *Apollo.*

When she was launched, Bond acquired in the 59-foot *Apollo* one of the fastest ocean racers ever designed and built in Australia.

Bond's version of the *Apollo* commission varies somewhat. He maintains he interviewed Miller for two days, liked what he saw, liked what he heard, then made another of the famous Bond judgments which turned out a winner. Whichever story one prefers, the two established a lasting relationship, a relationship that eventually led to the construction of *Southern Cross.*

But 38-year-old Robert Miller is clearly the stuff of which legends are made. Western Australia's yachting writer Bob Ross tells the story of how music-lover Miller hired a mariachi band from a third-rate Mexican bull ring while serving as an alternate on the Australian sailing squad for the 1968 Olympics at Acapulco. For the pure hell of it, Miller proceeded to conduct the discordant mob in the lobby of the plush Caletta Hotel as if he were Sir Bernard Heinze conducting the Melbourne Symphony Orchestra in Sydney's Opera House.

Play anything and Miller identifies it instantly. Turn on Sibelius' "Valse Triste" by the Philharmonia Orchestra conducted by Herbert Von Karajan and he'll blink his eyes and reply, "That's Herbert Von Karajan conducting the Philharmonia in the 'Valse Triste' by Sibelius, mate." According to syndicate manager Brian Leary, who himself knows Sibelius from Strauss, when it comes to identifying music, Miller's peers are few and unknown.

Apart from designing beautiful boats, Miller's other artistic talents extend to mobiles, which he builds no faster than one a year.

"At that rate, they're so rare," points out Miller, "that when I die they'll be as valuable as Picassos."

It is questionable, though, whether Picasso or any other artist would stand still while a young secretary sheared off his long forelocks with a pair of scissors. Yet Miller did. Miller stands well over six feet and weighs some fifteen stone (about 210 pounds), which used to make him perfect for hiking out on the trapeze of a Flying Dutchman, but rather than discouraging the fun-loving secretary with a left hook, Miller quietly remarked, "Ah, that's better, now I can see."

But never mistake Miller's peaceful giant image for fact. Miller fears few things that anyone has discovered. He and Bond get along famously and have sailed together as shipmates, but they have had their falling-outs as well. Reportedly, Miller became so furious with Bond one day that he ripped two telephones out of his Sydney office, broke a window and then, to his staff's horror, threatened to touch a match to the plans for *Southern Cross*. Picture taciturn Olin Stephens or gelid Britton Chance threatening to incinerate the drawings of *Courageous* or *Mariner,* if you will.

"I do get impatient," Miller agrees softly. His impatience, so he believes, is to blame for his doing so poorly as a light air sailor. In 1972, he won the Australian Soling Championship, then went on to win the Olympic trials for the class. His victories in both events in one of Australia's hottest classes were considered phenomenal and high hopes were held for him at the games. But Australia's daily semi-gales are not the zephyrs of Kiel and Miller finished a disappointing seventeenth in the Olympics.

"It was no one's fault but my own," he admitted later. "I get impatient in light air."

Still, impatience and passion are the prerogatives of genius and a natural born genius Miller truly is. Indeed, he is every bit as talented as his idols, L. Francis Herreshoff ("He was ingenious in all fields"), William Fife ("He designed boats that were more than good-looking, they were fast"), and G. L. Watson whose boats "were beautiful to look upon." How could Miller dare make such appraisals? Because his eye and intuition tells him so.

Like a great many yacht designers, Miller has next to no formal training in naval architecture but actually was trained to be a fitter and turner, a machinist. In truth, he dodged away from school so early that although he applied for jobs as a boatbuilder in yards that constructed lifeboats as well as shops that built rowing shells, none would touch him because he lacked a certificate from high school. Disappointed, Miller went to work for the railways as an apprentice machinist.

No cheap test exists for telling genius from dud in yacht architecture. A degree from the top-rated trade school won't do it. A set of promises won't do it either. In fact, the only way to uncover genius is to put up a great deal of money and have the novice's plans translated into a full-scale hull. If his boat overpowers other boats, or performs better, or looks more beautiful, then we have a new talent. If she flops . . . well, the aspiring designer may as well put away his tools and hopes for he will be a long time living down his reputation as a loser.

Fortunately, perhaps naturally, Miller escaped this route by following the only other course open to a budding genius. Without formality, he did what he wanted to do right from the beginning. He designed and built model boats.

Miller recalls that he put together his first boat at about age five. Shortly before, his grandmother had given him one of those top-heavy toy boats but he quickly tired of watching it being whipped by boats belonging to other youngsters whose fathers had built them model yachts to sail on the small lake near Newcastle, a couple of hours from Sydney. So Miller designed and built his own.

Cutting and gluing a handful of balsawood, he planked her into a super flyweight. The trouble was that she sailed as erratically as thistledown. Miller learned his first lesson in boat design.

As a result of that fiasco, he rebuilt the boat with a bit

of rocker to her keel and cut down her freeboard. Now running alongside in knee-deep water with U-control threads gripped fast, he steered his boat to win after win until he was tired of winning and left the lake for other fields.

Not school. He loathed school. Like Bond, school taught him nothing he needed to know about the beauty of boats or what made one boat sail faster than the next. He never took trigonometry and, as he looks back, his math marks were abysmal. On the other hand, the models and reading books by Uffa Fox and the understandable parts of Manfred Curry, whose incomprehensible hieroglyphics mostly mesmerized him, were giving Miller what he needed to know. At the same time, he hung around the fringes of sailing, borrowing boats sometimes, and hitching rides at other times, but always looking for answers to his questions.

At one time he also fooled with downwind sleds. These experimental freaks were ballasted with rocks and stepped their masts almost as far back as the transom. They were meant to do nothing but sail downhill forever and a day, and it may be that with those hell-for-breakfast sleds Miller began his reputation for designing boats whose prowess was all downwind. In any event, although still in his teens, Miller reached the stage where he felt ready to tackle his first full-scale boat, one that would go both ways — upwind as well as down.

Apart from fascination with downwind performance, Miller's other fetish is lightness. The 20-footer he put together in his back yard from plans that consisted of nothing more explicit than the sketches in one of Uffa Fox's books, was ultra light, but not as much out of his hang-up about weight as because, as an impoverished apprentice fitter and turner for the railways, he couldn't afford any more than the bare essentials. When he poured the lead keel, a minor disaster occurred: the mold exploded, largely because of skimping in the forms. Then, when anyone asked him why his boat lacked frames, he would reply archly, "Because it's worked out scientifically," but today he admits that it was as much a matter of cost. Inch by inch, he learned and when he finally launched the shell, she proved terribly fast in light air . . . to the amazement of everyone, save Miller. She also fell apart so often, he spent as much time fitting her back together as he did sailing.

When Miller joined Australia's 18-footer wars he finally began to attract the public eye. Eighteen-foot skiffs, or skiffies, as they are affectionately known, are those acorn-sized craft that whistle about the waters of Australia and New Zealand beneath clouds of sail with crews of wild men swinging from side to side on trapezes to counter the tremendous sail pressures. Miller designed and built an 18-footer he named *Taipan,* after the highly poisonous Australian snake but, unlike her namesake, she bit no one except Miller with loss after loss until he began to lose his famous patience.

With his next skiff, he revolutionized the class. That boat carried a three-man crew for the first time, all of whom were strung out on trapezes. She also was designed with a hard chine — a V-hull — another departure. No skiff-watcher in Sydney or anywhere else had seen a boat quite like *Venom.* Nor had anyone seen a boat go quite as fast. She sailed so swiftly that the punters, who bet on skiffies, began shouting "cheater" in her wake. But a cheater she wasn't, and Miller came away from Brisbane with the world championship in his bag. It was enough for him. He turned to crewing a 19-foot Flying Dutchman.

Sailing with Craig Whitworth, the two won the Australian Flying Dutchman Championship the following year. During that year, Miller and Whitworth, realize it or not, found themselves melding into a strong team. Both already had established reputations as sailmakers, but that year proved to them both that calm, cool and collected Whitworth provided a perfect foil for the volcanic Miller, who endlessly spouts ideas in every direction. The next move seemed preordained. In an abandoned dance hall at Spit Junction in Sydney, they set up business as Miller & Whitworth, Sailmakers. Their reputation soon spread and one success led to another. Miller continued to design boats as well as cut sails, and in 1967 drafted the 16-foot Contender, which the International Yacht Racing Union accepted as an International Class, giving it instant status world-wide.

At the same time, Miller's reputation as a yacht doctor who knew how to help an owner make his boat go faster, developed solidly, but no one yet was willing to risk his designing a big boat from scratch. Even so, ocean racing designs sprang from his board almost in a continuous stream, but all went unbuilt. Then a man named Ted Kaufman, for whom Miller had crewed aboard a Star boat years earlier, turned up with a request that Miller help him design a 40-foot ocean racer to be named *Mercedes III*. Kaufman drew the profile for his new boat while Miller produced the lines, including the shape of her keel, which turned out a thing of joy to Miller's technical way of thinking. Furthermore, like all happy rags-to-riches endings, *Mercedes III* became a sensation and Miller had his first real boost on the long climb to a stable design career and the twelve-meter. Thus, Miller was more than a little prepared when Bond came along with his order for the 59-foot *Apollo* for the 1970 Bermuda Race.

Bond describes Miller this way:

"Miller is one of those chaps you really can believe in because he is so completely sure of himself and is so clear and convinced in his objectives. He probably has done more practical sailing in his early years than any other yacht designer. In other words, he's so practical about what he's going to do, you have to feel confident in him."

The practical, yet artistic, Miller doesn't keep track of

such things, but he thinks that fifteen designs have unrolled from his desk since Kaufman's boat, including a 46-footer named *Ginkgo* which later was to form a tenuous tie-in with *Southern Cross.* Long, narrow, spartan, untested by tank, that wooden-hulled sloop was another striking departure from the norm in ocean racing design. Flush decked to the last line of her stern, she followed Miller's developing philosophy of design with her big shoulders and slim hips and she combined a completely distinctive appearance with fearsome bursts of speed.

In her first middle-distance race, *Ginkgo* won, then went on to take four out of five test races to easily earn a berth on the Australian Admiral's Cup team. In the process, she also had whipped the most recent boats from the boards of Sparkman & Stephens, the American designers whose reputation for fast ocean racers is legendary. That pleased Miller. There were some Australians, too, who couldn't be blamed for regarding *Ginkgo* as an omen of spring.

Next, Miller designed a second *Apollo* for Alan Bond. She turned out almost as well as *Ginkgo,* although she was a heavier sistership, built of aluminum to unusually heavy scantlings. The pair made their mark, as the overall Admiral's Cup standings show. Sailed in British waters, the Admiral's Cup had *Ginkgo* fourth and *Apollo* sixth out of forty-one boats in the world's most prestigious ocean team race. And Miller's reputation moved up another rung.

Even so, more than one Australian asked why pick "an offbeat genius," as the Australian press likes to call Miller, to design a challenger when he could offer not a scrap of experience in creating twelve-meters?

The answer was simple, according to Bond when he explained how Miller got the commission to design *Southern Cross.* As Bond tells it, he asked Miller one question: "Would you like to win the America's Cup?"

"His reaction to that settled the matter because I want people who need to win," Bond related. "Miller then was still relatively unknown and consequently he could gain the most out of it. He's the kind of person I need associated with this challenge — not people who know defeat, but people who need to win."

Miller wasted no time in going to work. In a way his methods of designing go back to earlier days and are far simpler than the techniques most often used now with their heavy dependence on computers and test tanks. Miller depends on his eye, just as did Herreshoff, Fife and the others, but, like Herreshoff, he also is thoroughly trained working with his hands. Miller knows what is and what is not practicable as well as workable, mechanically.

In any event, his basic aim was to design a boat that, as he puts it, "would be good downwind but not at the expense of making her a dud to weather." She would be a narrow twelve with about the same displacement and draft as previous twelves. In other words, she would draw about 9.3 feet, have a beam of about twelve feet, and she would have a U-shaped entry at the bow to allay any tendency toward hobbyhorsing — that death-dealing up and down pitching motion that digs a grave for any boat, but which has been the hallmark of more than one of the recent twelves. Too, she would be designed to go best in about 12 to 15 knots of wind or, as Miller calls it, "lightish stuff."

Miller has little faith in computers. If the computer says one thing and his eye shows him another, he believes his eye. "I've not had that much computer time," Miller mused. "I don't understand the things."

But he does understand the test tank in which scale model boats of preliminary plans are tested to answer the designer's questions. After all, they are only more refined and sophisticated extensions of those models Miller had built and sailed as a youngster. Alan Bond donated $13,000 to the University of Sydney's test tank, but Miller's use of the tank was sporadic when compared to others in his profession.

He towed five models, including one of *Gretel II* with a keel configuration that closely resembled the one he planned for *Southern Cross.* To his delight, the thin, short fin made *Gretel's* model perform better than before. As a yardstick, he also had wangled a model of *Intrepid* as she originally was built before Britton Chance redesigned her for the 1970 Cup defense. By comparison, *Southern Cross* outperformed her quite satisfactorily. Still Miller doesn't believe that the tank always provides the last answer, and when it comes down to it, he again will trust his eye and feelings first. When he put *Southern Cross'* final model through her paces in the tank, the results were most heartening in the scaled 12 to 15 knot winds, but when wind velocities were increased, the model's performance slipped sharply.

Such results might nibble away at any designer's confidence, and it could be that they were some of the reason that Miller told Bond he didn't think Australia stood a hope in hell as a challenger, but they didn't stop him. *Southern Cross* was built as designed, the tank notwithstanding.

Then, in one of her early tests after launching, *Southern Cross* was sent out in a breeze of wind substantially heavier than any she likely will encounter at Newport — in fact, heavy enough that a race most probably would be called — and despite being outfitted in an ill-cut, baggy new suit of sails (made, ironically, by Miller & Whitworth), she sailed upwind as stiffly as the Tour Eiffel and returned, as every Miller boat does, skating silkenly downwind. Miller's pleasure in the sight was apparent, but mixed in with it was a touch of "I told you so."

While Miller and a staff of five worked on the hull plans, young John Bertrand designed her rig. John Bertrand holds a master's degree from Massachusetts Institute of Technology, is a graduate engineer in aerodynamics, and is one of the few Australians with twelve-meter experience to gain Bond's nod, having acted as *Gretel II's* boss in charge of headsails and spinnakers during her battle with *Intrepid.* He also researched American twelve-meters while in the United States; represented Australia in the single-handed Finn Class at the 1972 Olympics (fourth), and at the World Championships (second). In short, Bertrand is a well-rounded, highly skilled expert in anything to do with the spars and rigging and no mean sailor. With the assistance of John Blackler — a specialist in the design of helicopter blades — he produced some of the cleanest, most delicate and apparently most efficient aluminum spars to come out of the southern *or* the northern hemispheres.

Dismasting is an accepted risk in tuning up a Cup boat, so when one day *Southern Cross'* spar came tumbling down, the crew merely said "Heigh ho," repaired the mast with a sleeve and soon were out sailing again.

Miller does share Bond's contention that the Australians are at a distinct disadvantage as challengers, but for different reasons. He sees — matter of factly — the Americans as age-old, big boat sailors with armies of big boat sailors from which to draw crew candidates. He feels their ability to design and build boats like twelve-meters is second to none, thanks again to tradition and experience.

"We're small boat sailors down here with scant experience in any of those departments," he observed simply.

But who will deny that it is this lopsidedness, this lofty inequity that makes the America's Cup the special challenge it is?

For his part, Bond is convinced that Miller earned his handsome fee, but neither he nor Miller will say what it was. "I think Bob has done what he set out to do — designed a boat with a little speed," Bond said one morning while staring out over the Indian Ocean at

Yanchep. "There's no question that she's a fast boat, and I think she's very simple and very easy to handle compared to *Gretel II*. In fact, I think she's basically in keeping with the man himself."

Miller's opinion is more guarded. When asked to rate the importance of crew and skipper against that of the boat, he answered, "The hull is more important than the rig unless the weather is very light, but overall the boat is less important than the crew and the skipper."

There are few who would argue, particularly remembering such dramatic instances as the day that little, gnome-like C. Sherman Hoyt pulled the American chestnuts from the fire in the 1934 Cup tilt between *Rainbow* and her plainly faster British rival *Endeavour*. There it was skipper, crew and helmsman who clearly saved the day despite an inferior boat.

And there probably are few who realize that truth more clearly than a tough, single-minded, optometrist from Brisbane named John Cuneo, or the easy-going, wine-merchant from Sydney known as "Gentleman Jim" Hardy.

Southern Cross *has dual steering wheels, low slung boom, and easy-to-work deck controls.*

The crew prepare for a training match. Nosecap protects bow and is removed when racing.

Slam and thrash, the main goes up after being towed out of Yanchep Marina.

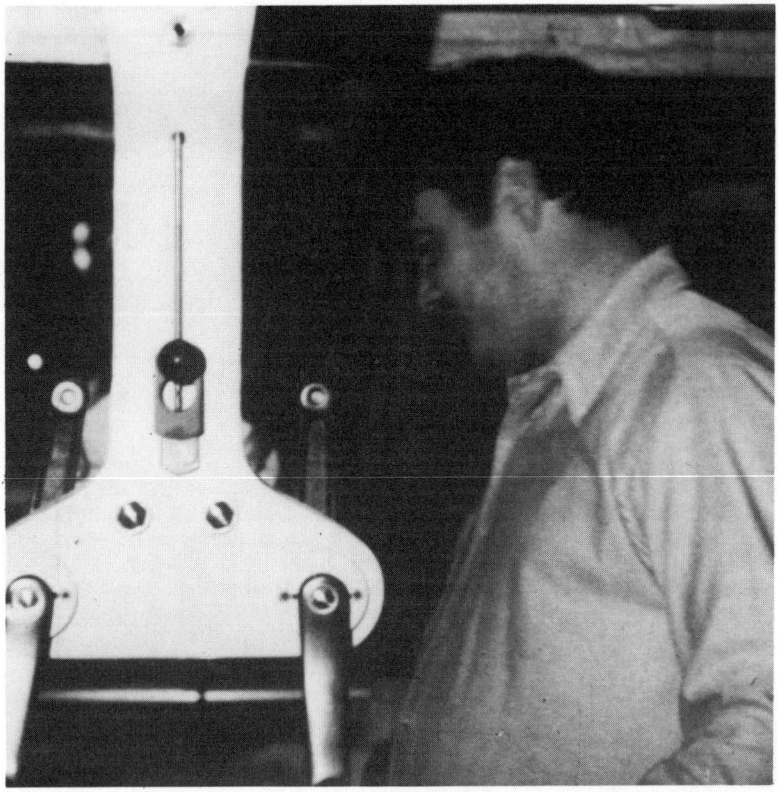

Designer Bob Miller checks one of the winch grinders under the deck of Southern Cross.

All sails rap full, Southern Cross *slips along.*

John Cuneo and Jim Hardy.

12
KA4

Wheels and Buttons

ANYONE WHO HAS MESSED ABOUT in yachting for any time at all soon learns that there are as many ways to skipper a boat as there are skippers. Each skipper reacts to command in his own way and the extremes are far apart. At one end of the scale is the lion, the so-called Captain Bligh type—misnamed though the type may be. The Blighs are prone to yelling, peremptorily shouting orders right and left, and trying to do every job themselves, expecting little from their crews other than their weight on the halyard or the sheets. At the other end is the mild man, the lamb, whose lack of color never has earned him a generic name, a man who prefers to leave everything to his crew from sweepdown to steering, to tactical decisions and who simply goes along for the ride and to pay the bills. In between, is every shade and grade, but no matter what, it is the captain who must accept the responsibility of command. It is he who receives the trophy at the end of a successful race, and he who endures the pitying looks and often the vilification if his boat comes last. In Cup racing, this truth is especially evident.

Not so evident, though, is just where in the scale of skippers lies the best man for a given task and there is no iron-bound answer—skippers all through the spectrum have done the job at one time or another. Take even the case of Emil "Bus" Mosbacher, whose name is nearly legendary as a Cup skipper but who is something of an anomaly, being both a lamb and a lion. Ashore his considerable social graces made him Chief of Protocol for the United States State Department for a time, but afloat he is a demanding perfectionist who on more than one occasion drew bitter complaints from his crew.

Still, the question of picking a skipper proved Bond's most nettling problem, and even as *Southern Cross* and *Gretel* were made ready for the long sea voyage to Newport in April of 1974, the final answer was yet to come, and in a way, the battle had just been joined between John Cuneo, a tense, nervy and skilled small boat sailor, and easygoing Jim Hardy, who also had come from the class boat ranks but had been skipper and chief factotum of *Gretel II's* campaign in 1970, and as such was the most experienced twelve-meter match man in the *Southern Cross* camp.

Bond had started out bravely enough naming Cuneo, a Brisbane optometrist, as *Southern Cross'* skipper, following his pattern of wanting only winners who bore no taint of losing, even though Cuneo was a dark horse in many ways. But he had qualities that Bond was seeking because, even more than Bond, or more than Miller, Cuneo hated to lose. He was known up and down the waterfront for sailing a deadly serious race, and usually those races finished in his favor. From the time he began sailing at the age of eight, he had won seven Australian Sharpie titles, two Dragon championships, and a Five-O-Five championship. That record ignored a number of close calls, like a fifth at the Acapulco Olympics in 1968, although he had made up for that failure by taking the Gold Medal in the Dragons at the Kiel Olympics in 1970. As a fresh winner, Cuneo seemed to be Bond's man.

But Cuneo wasn't without problems. As a small boat sailor, he was at home with a tiller but had little experience with a steering wheel. There is a difference, as sailors know, but not an insurmountable one. Perhaps more significantly, Cuneo's experience had been almost entirely in the multi-boat class contests and he knew little of the fine points of the two-boat match race which is quite another fish weir. In fact, in his single experience with match racing in the American Congressional Cup matches off Long Beach in California in 1972, he had come in a disheartening tenth in the ten-boat contest, having won but one of the round-robin matches.

These, though, were problems that Bond felt could be overcome with ease in the long training program that had been laid out for *Southern Cross* and her crew. A carefully programmed regimen was established at the outset. Before the launching of *Southern Cross,* Cuneo sailed *Gretel I,* or *G-1* as she was called in the camp, against *Gretel II. G-2* was detuned to hold her back within range of the older, slower *G-1* with the idea of keeping the vital practice in starts close, hard and realistic. After *Southern Cross* was launched, Cuneo took her over and *G-2* was tuned up to make her as fast or faster than in her salad days off Newport.

At the same time, a card of sparring partners was assembled for Cuneo. To wring him out, keep him off balance, and to prevent his becoming accustomed to the nuances and tricks of a single opponent, a variety of skippers came to Sun City from Australia as well as overseas. The list included David Forbes, the Australian Olympic Gold Medalist in Stars; John Bertrand, whom we already have met; the Australian big boat expert and sailmaker Hughie Treharne, and Jim Hardy, who was scheduled to provide the final polish.

From overseas, Andy Rose was invited from the United States following the 1973 Congressional Cup races. An easy-going match racing wizard with a wide sleeve full of tricks, Rose has had a wealth of match racing experience in the Congressional Cups as a crewman for Argyl Campbell who won it in 1972. Campbell, himself, was invited but declined on the grounds of patriotism.

Leading the band was Bill Lucas, who owned *Panamuna* before Bond and is noted for his spartan approach to big boat racing. He takes along a three-man crew, a handful of candy bars, and a stock of dirty stories. Lucas claims that a good three-man crew can cope with any boat; they can live on the candy bars, and the dirty stories are designed to keep them warm. Zany though his approach to racing may be, the irrepressible Lucas nevertheless has managed to capture every bit of silverware lying around loose in Western Australia.

Lucas today claims he never will forget the first practice round on the waters off Yanchep. *G-1* and *G-2* met at the line, and after circling each other in the classic ritual which usually precedes each match race start, Lucas looked up to find *G-1* charging straight at him as if bent on spearing *G-2*. At the same instant, he realized Cuneo had no intention of giving way.

"I wasn't going to ram twelve-meters, but John didn't seem to feel quite the same way," Lucas recalled later. "It was then that I really found out Cuneo was treating the whole thing extremely seriously."

But just how seriously no one appreciated until the day the two twelves collided at a combined speed of about fourteen knots just after the ten minute gun warned of another skirmish. Each of the twelves weighs roughly thirty tons and when they met head-on, the collision spun *G-2* around like a toy, and sent *G-1* swerving towards the starting boat which scrambled out of the way.

Over the two-way radio serving the three boats crackled a querulous voice calling Cuneo from the start boat:

"What're yer want to do now?" Unmistakably, the voice had in mind returning to the dock to cool off.

Came back Cuneo curtly, "What do you mean 'What're yer want to do now?' We got four minutes to the starting gun. Get cracking!"

All that remains of the crash today is a foot-long splinter of wood hanging on the wall in Cuneo's Yanchep office. Painted on one side is a legend which reads, "This is what happens when Bill Lucas gets too close."

Hughie Treharne, though, was responsible for a proper nose-job on *G-2*. Unaccustomed to a twelve-meter's amazing powers of acceleration, he rammed *G-1* so hard during one practice go that he pounded in a good foot of *G-2's* bow. Shipwrights replaced the wood mush with a temporary and unsightly strip of aluminum to carry the forestay.

There were other bangs and bumps that measured the Sun City combat temperature with almost everyone thinking, "The hotter the better." By the time *Southern Cross* arrived on the scene with a precautionary length of rubber tire lashed to her razor-sharp stem, *G-1* and *G-2* had been involved in ten major collisions.

The practice courses off Yanchep invariably were laid out as windward-leeward legs of about four-and-a-half miles each. The beats and runs were closely contested and, as training progressed, Cuneo began to show signs of progress that almost silenced those who still questioned whether he had been the right choice. Much of the time the boats completed four or five races each day, but on one memorable day when the weather was better than perfect, they squeezed in no less than nine races of nine miles each.

The reason for the short courses rather than the standard America's Cup course of twenty-four miles was simply compression. The shorter the course, the more concentrated the competition. Decisions speed up, crew work is distilled, maneuvering has to be concise, and errors are magnified. And there was no let-down. The practice matches were contested almost as if the America's Cup rode on the outcome of each one.

"It was so serious and so tough, we would return to the harbor physically, as well as emotionally, drained at the end of each day," Bill Lucas recalled while reporting on the early training sesions, and then went on to tell the story of one memorable day that, perhaps more than most, was almost prophetic of problems to come.

It was a beautiful day and Bill Lucas stood at *Gretel II's* helm poised for his next brush with Cuneo. Cuneo was in difficulties. The jib on *G-1* had split from luff to leach as she maneuvered for the start, leaving her about as manageable as an overloaded barge. At the first signs of the rip, Cuneo's crew had sprung to change sails only to be ordered back by the tough, glowering Cuneo who, although hopelessly on the defensive, saw no reason to give the start away to *G-2* because of a torn headsail as others might have done. Letting it be known to everyone within a mile that, "The first one who touches that jib, I'll bloody well brain," he brought *G-1* about on the starboard tack and with the right of way and just as he had done before, he took precise aim at *G-2*.

In a split second, aggressor had become defender and to escape another collision, *G-2* was forced to tack quickly away, fouling her sheet in the process so that her genoa was strapped aback like a huge brake. As they battled to free the sheet on *G-2,* Cuneo slipped *G-1* across the line, changed his torn jib, and blithely sailed away from his floundering opponent.

"He's utterly ruthless, utterly dedicated, and utterly tough," one of the crewmen observed precisely and a bit more than ruefully, and added, "If there is a problem, it's going to be the skipper. He's too tough on the crew."

At Christmas time "Gentleman Jim" Hardy showed up at Yanchep to rub down the rough edges of Cuneo's match-racing technique. By no stretch of the imagination is Gentleman Jim a troublemaker unless, that is, you hand him a boat. Then, as Bob Miller once put it, "You'd better stay out of his way."

Tall and strong as wire, the forty-year-old Hardy has the rangy build of an oarsman which, indeed, he once was in his school days. Gentleman Jim was raised on the water by a family of sailors which included his father who died in a plane crash when Hardy was five. Before his death the senior Hardy owned the yawl *Nerida* which later won the Sydney-Hobart race under another owner. And Hardy's mother, as well as a pair of older brothers, all sail as does his wife, Anne, and his sons, David and Richard, who know the difference between a jib and a staysail.

At the tender age of ten, Hardy took to the water in a woebegone twelve-footer named *Mermaid.* At the same time, he discovered the many books on sails, sailing and even the America's Cup, never dreaming that one day he would sail a Cup boat himself. *Mermaid* gave way to a Cadet class boat named *Nocroo* as Hardy's sailing skills sharpened. Far from a simple boat to build even for experienced boatbuilders, Hardy nonetheless built *Nocroo* himself despite having yet to reach his thirteenth birthday. With her he became runner-up in the Cadet championship, establishing a reputation for finishing second that was to dog him right into his *Southern Cross* days when his original application was turned down in favor of Cuneo because he had finished second to *Intrepid* in 1970. Bond, you will remember, wanted winners.

There were occasions when Hardy won, though. At nineteen, he built himself into a different class with the twelve square meter sharpie, *T. M. Hardy.* Time after time, he finished second in the National Championships —three times being beaten by Cuneo—until finally he laughed the last laugh in 1959. That was the year Cuneo lost the championship to him in a hard fought series.

In later years, he switched from class to class in search of excellence. One regatta he would sail a Finn singlehanded, next he would be at the tiller of a Five-O-Five. He attended the Tokyo Olympics as alternate in the Flying Dutchman, having once again finished second in the trials to pick an Australian representative. He travelled the world looking for the ultimate victory.

When the Five-O-Five World Championships came to Adelaide, Hardy came close to his goal. Sailing stars from the far corners of the world were on hand, including the master himself, the Great Dane, Paul Elvstrom. It was the opportunity of a lifetime for Hardy to heart-spike his second place jinx and in his own methodical, quiet way, Gentleman Jim made the most of it. Not only did he win the World's, but he had the satisfaction of nudging Elvstrom, who many say is the greatest sailor in the world, into that customary old slot of second.

Soon after achieving this high point in his sailing career, veteran sailor Gordon Ingate introduced Hardy to twelve-meter sailing aboard *Gretel I* in her abortive attempt to defeat *Dame Pattie* for the right to challenge for the America's Cup in 1967. To hear Hardy tell it, it was a case of love at first touch, and when 1970 and the *Gretel II* campaign rolled around, Hardy became the popular choice to take command.

Few will forget the series he sailed against the French in the first Cup challenge eliminations. He beat them in four straight races. Still fewer will forget the furor created by the famous protest during the start of the second race when *Gretel II* lost a certain victory through disqualification. The story made headlines around the world, and in Australia tempers flared. Officially, the record states *Intrepid* successfully defended the Cup, four victories to one, and with the first part of that statement, Hardy agrees. He disagrees, however, with the score. In his book, *Intrepid* didn't win four-one, she won three-two.

An article in the magazine "Sail" best summed up the turmoil in Hardy's soul after that debacle, in which the New York Yacht Club acted not only as victim, but as judge, jury, and executioner as well. "I will never until my dying day be able to understand how a windward yacht can come charging in at any angle, bounce off a leeward yacht, get a two-minute advantage, lose the race because the other boat sailed a better race, and then be awarded it all on a protest," Hardy was quoted as saying and then added, "I couldn't in my wildest dreams see how he (*Intrepid's* skipper Bill Ficker) could sustain a 42.1 (e) against us. I said to Martin (Martin Visser, a member of *Gretel II's* afterguard and a back-up helmsman) 'If they get out of this one, I'll get out of sailing.' "

Yet they did and he didn't, for now we find him battling for the wheel of a new Cup contender, and with some by-advantages that no one else on the *Southern Cross* team can match. Hardy knows Newport. And the waters off Brenton Reef. He knows the New York Yacht Club's peccadillos, and has been tested before by the atmosphere that swirls along the waterfront off Thames Street. The long tow out, and the tensions are old hat to Gentleman Jim, and he would be geared to ease his crew over the jitters that infest every challenger just before the first start.

Before he left for Sun City, Hardy had privately confided to a close friend that he would like nothing better than to take command of *Southern Cross,* and that he intended to do his best to get that command. But the prospects seemed dim when he began to sail *Gretel II* against Cuneo in *Southern Cross* because the polishing plan was going exactly according to the carefully drawn program. Although suffering from severe teething pangs, *Southern Cross* won more often than she lost, especially on those days when light airs paid Sun City a visit.

Thus as the long Australian summer waned and the time came to ready *Southern Cross* and *Gretel* for their month-long voyage aboard a freighter to Newport, Bond and Syndicate Manager Leary faced one of the most difficult decisions of the campaign. Bond, who has learned to recognize his mistakes as well as enjoy his successes, had to admit that perhaps selecting a skipper solely on his drive to win wasn't enough, and that even a concentrated year of training might not convert a small boat sailor into a skilled match-racing skipper. There was little doubt that Gentleman Jim's long experience in three twelve-meter campaigns had given him an edge, but there still were questions of what effect the vacation from sailing would have on crew and skippers as they moved the operation half way around the world.

There was one answer to the problem: *Southern Cross* would go to Newport with two skippers and there the final question would be solved during the three-months plus that remained before the real battle for the America's Cup began.

So *Southern Cross* enjoyed a plethora of skippers at the end of the Down Under summer as she left Yanchep for the wars, but there was even one more skipper, although this one was one fashioned from wire, resistors and transistors, and spoke only when punched. Officially called a computer, but familiarly known as "Fred," the black box was another of those electronic marvels that have been added to sail racing when cost is no object to lend the breathing skipper a hand in analyzing the myriad factors that go into the best tune and the best trim of his boat. Fred can supply answers faster and more accurately than any member of any afterguard, including Bus Mosbacher, and as a gauge of his worth, Fred came high. The machine cost $12,000 and the complex problem of programming it another $18,000 to set Bond back some $30,000 Australian.

Essentially, wires were led to shrouds and other critical points in the boat to record rig tensions, but Fred also could tell what sail combination to set for any point of sailing according to wind speed and direction. Lest there be a mistake, the answer was printed by stylus on a board. "Spinnaker, genoa, mainsail," and so forth, Fred said, down to the last comma.

Fred also determined the exact mast bend for any given condition and in his spare time provided the precise times to tack on wind shifts, when to jibe while tacking down wind, and the best course to the next mark. In short, Fred tells *Southern Cross'* navigator, Jack Baxter, X, Y, and Zed.

Some skippers look on Fred and his ilk with arched eyebrows, feeling that such gadgets threaten to take the art out of sailing, although both Cuneo and Hardy found that Fred had his uses if you knew how to talk to him. But whatever, Fred was another example that the *Southern Cross* campaign wasn't leaving a single stone on the beach unturned in their effort to take the America's Cup from its case, and even as the final crews were being selected, Fred already had established himself as a permanent member . . . not breathing, not complaining, but thinking in a flash.

John Cuneo and Jim Hardy sailed many tough races off Yanchep.

Veteran Jim Hardy is eager for a chance on the helm of Southern Cross *to revenge his 1970 Cup defeat.*

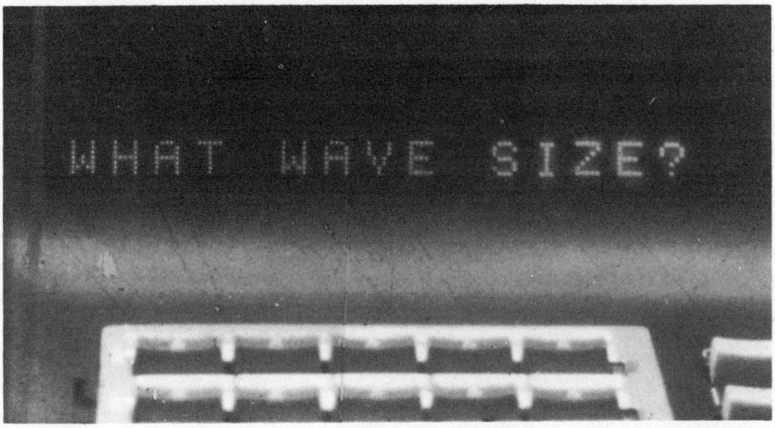

Before giving a computed decision, "Fred" asks for a wave measurement.

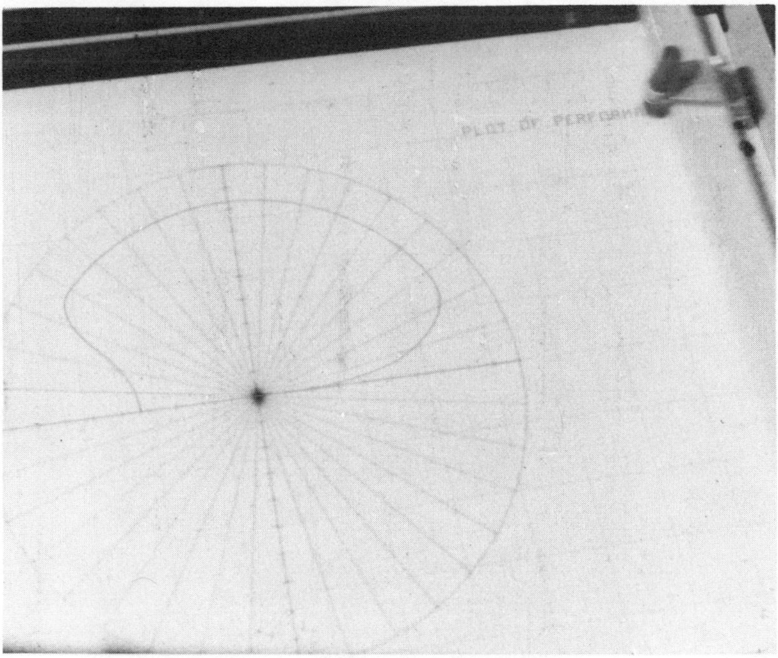

Given the desired course, wind, and sea conditions, the computer prints out a performance plot using various sail combinations.

The crew of Southern Cross.

12

KA4

No Bludgers Here

ONE SUNDAY MORNING in late November of 1973 in the boatshed at Yanchep, the time arrived to select the crewmen who would go overseas with Australia's challenge for the America's Cup from the crewmen who would be left behind. It was a tense hour in the dark, drafty cavern, presided over by the almost gloomily solemn board of selectors which included, of course, Alan Bond, the prime mover; John Cuneo, skipper of *Southern Cross;* John Bertrand, tactician, and Brian Leary, the syndicate manager. At the outset, there was little joshing because everyone knew that some friend was to be hurt.

The crewmen who were to be left behind had worked or sailed on the *Gretels* for weeks, and it is not difficult to imagine the depth of their disappointments when their names did not come up. On the other hand, it is equally easy to imagine the euphoria induced when Bond called out the names of those who were to accompany *Southern Cross* and *Gretel II* to Newport.

In the ranks of the happy were six men from the state of Western Australia, Bond's home state, three from New South Wales, two from Queensland, and one each from Victoria and the island of Tasmania. Although two over the twelve-meter crew limit of eleven men, one of the hands on the list was Alan Bond, who will step in or out depending on how the campaign progresses, while the last and thirteenth man will serve as a wild card substitute.

Professions and occupations ran the gamut. Alan Bond was a business tycoon. John Cuneo, an optometrist. As an aeronautical engineer, John Bertrand answered to the nickname "Aero." John Shaw had been crew for Cuneo — few of the crew had been shipmates prior to *Southern Cross* — when they won their Gold Medal at Kiel. He was a shipwright by trade. Another shipwright was Norman Hyett. Both Jack Baxter, the navigator, and foredeck boss John "Chink" Longley were schoolteachers, while Christopher Willing practiced law. Jim Hardy was a New South Wales wine maker. Les Valmadre was an architect, Lee Killingworth held a degree in business management, and Graeme Johnson was a student architect. Finally, Robert "Rat" Sterling was a New South Wales farmer when he wasn't earning his soubriquet by hanging around the world's wharves looking for a berth on an ocean racer.

After that painful hour in the boatshed, they all piled into cars and drove down to Bond's home outside Dalkeith, a suberb of Perth, where Bond threw an unforgettable party. Almost everyone made a speech before the day was over which, according to those who were there, were in one of three veins — humorous, serious or seriocomic. As the refreshment flowed, so did the party until it reached the vast pool. Before long people started swimming and it wasn't much later that every man-jack leapt into the pool, with or without swimming trunks, including the steward who dove in still decked out in white jacket and black bow tie. As a safety-valve to reduce the pressure, Bond's party was a masterpeice.

Out of the crew on *Southern Cross,* all but three are Cup boat rookies. John Bertrand who, as a member of the Miller & Whitworth firm almost came with the boat, had been, as mentioned earlier, chief of *Gretel II's* headsail department. Norm Hyett was aboard the first *Gretel* in 1962, and Rat Sterling served aboard *G-2* in 1970. Both Rat and Hyett were signed on for the Australian effort while aboard the American sloop *Sorcery* during the 1973 Admiral's Cup in Britain. The rest of the crew came over the transom, but each had to meet one stringent requirement. As Bond put it: "Our selection was based on lads who turned up with their kit bags and said, 'Look, I reckon I'm pretty good and I'd like to be a part of the campaign. Will you give me a go?' That always was a good beginning and after that we needed to determine only, did the man really want to win? Was he prepared to give up everything? After all, it's the same thing."

Not every conscript demonstrated complete dedication and two were sacked. They were prepared to do what they considered necessary to win the Cup but, as Bond observed, it wasn't everything they had. It was certain death for a man to attempt reserving for himself even an hour a day. Bond demanded 100 percent devotion to the campaign with absolutely no reservations.

"The Americans have always had that 100 percent effort," Bond explained, "now I think we have it."

But Bond also realized that such devotion is a two-way street, and he carefully avoided the mistake Sir Frank Packer had made in Australia's first challenge in 1962. Sir Frank had hoped at the time that by with-holding his selection of the final crew to the last possible moment, he could key up the crew to the point of super-competition. Instead, he bred nothing but confusion and resentment aboard the first *Gretel.* On *Southern Cross,* the crew knew early in the game exactly where they stood which did nothing to harm that intangible devotion as well as provided that much more time for developing compatibility and the essential teamwork.

No less a factor in preserving that dedication and devotion was Bond's ruling that there would be absolutely no interference in the skipper and crew decisions on tactics. Sir Frank had made that mistake, too, and in one of the 1962 races his off-the-boat "advisory committee" had insisted that Jock Sturrock set a heavy mainsail despite Sturrock's protests that a lighter sail was in order. The wind that day remained light, proving Sturrock right, and *Gretel* blew the race. *Southern Cross* from the outset, would not be badgered by morale-eroding second guessing.

And the endless practice that was the *Southern Cross* crew's destiny, was designed not only to provide the skills needed, but also to establish that crew confidence without which no boat can win. The ill-fated Australian campaign in 1970 showed to both Bond and Cuneo that half measures would not be effective. That crew had demonstated a cool excellence when *Gretel II* met *France,* but when they came up against *Intrepid,* they seemed shellshocked and inept.

"As we went into the first race with *Intrepid,*" skipper Jim Hardy later reported to writer Bob Ross, "everyone had the jitters. It turned out to be a very grim day all over." It is Cuneo's contention that aboard *Southern Cross* sufficient training would calm jitters and brighten grim days before they dawned.

There was one final lesson. Should *Southern Cross* ultimately lose, there would be no repetition of the denunciations that flew back and forth from designer to skipper to sailmaker to crew after the *Dame Pattie* loss. Recriminations did not atone for a loss. Everyone would try his damndest to keep his mouth shut. Not for that reason alone, but for reasons of security, too, each man working or sailing on the boats voluntarily signed a pledge of secrecy which read:

"I hereby agree that during all the time I am associated in any way with the 1974 America's Cup Challenge either as a crew member sailing in or associated with the Cup challenging twelve-meters, crewing *Offsider* or any other tender or vessel, or engaged in any other duties afloat or ashore, I will not supply any information or photographs relating to the 1974 America's Cup Challenge to the press, radio, or television or for any other purpose, either in writing or by word of mouth, without the approval of the Cup Challenge public relations consultant, R. C. Hemery or his agents.

"I realize any breach of this agreement will result in my immediate dismissal from any participation in the 1974 America's Cup Challenge.

"I further undertake that I will make no statements relating to the 1974 America's Cup Challenge, nor provide photographs or information, whether written or by word of mouth or by any other means for a period of three months after the conclusion of my participation in the America's Cup Challenge."

Each man signed that comprehensive document in due solemnity.

Meanwhile, to handle the press Bond hired the eminently talented communications expert R. C. "Bob" Hemery of Perth. Hemery would accompany the team to Newport. "Early on it was decided that all statements from the Australian camp would emanate only from Alan Bond and Manager Brian Leary. We're going to have a constant line response to the media without team members being subjected to outside pressures," said Hemery, a Perth City Councillor and old ally of Bond's. "We want the crew's one hundred percent attention to win the Cup. They can save their comments until after the victory celebrations."

From eight a.m. when the Doberman was kenneled to six p.m. when he came on duty again, the atmosphere at Yanchep felt electric. With Thursdays their only day off, the crews sailed every weekend. From Monday to Friday, though, it mostly was weld this, fix that, alter the other thing, as they hustled to maintain and refine the boats. To lighten *G-2,* they ripped out a bulkhead and the head.

Southern Cross gave them headaches from the start, as any new boat and certainly any revolutionary boat will. On her first run, her novel winches broke down and had to be returned to designer Malcolm Barlow in Sydney. Chains had jumped off the sprocket teeth on the coffee grinders and bigger sprockets were ordered.

Miller's layout of the boat created a few problems. When they began to sail her, crewmen decided that several alterations were needed to make the layout more workable and efficient. They realigned the winch-pumper platforms and beefed up the hull with aluminum hanging knees when the vang began to buckle the deck. Bang, bang, bang went the tempo.

"What is this?" Jim Hardy marveled the day he arrived to begin polishing up Cuneo. "It looks like an army camp around here."

While maintenance went on below, up in the sail-loft others were re-cutting sails or testing them on the horizontal mast. A large graph was hung on the wall charting spinnaker handling times during practice rounds. Drops averaged fifteen seconds; hoists, ten seconds; gybes, ten seconds. No room for complaint there.

Everyone lived on the site in the chalets provided by Bond at Sun City, but the crew saw little of their temporary homes. Even the mid-day break meant ten minutes over a box lunch in the Yanchep lounge with its long table full of "Playboy" and sailing magazines, and then it was back to work. Still, the crew thrived on the routine and finally drew an accolade from their single-minded skipper who proudly announced one day:

"There're no bludgers here."

A bludger is an Australian term for a slacker, a goof-off.

Cuneo does hold one theory that, among sailors particularly, could set up basic friction. He believes that hard work, hard sailing and hard smoking and drinking do not mix. That he persuaded his Cup crew to cut down on both in the interests of the challenge was a ticklish mission at best, but Cuneo succeeded and they did. There are Australians who still don't believe it.

At sea, training meant sail, sail, and sail until the tension between the two racing crews reached such heights that it was nearly palpable and became almost frightening. Several times, after particularly close matches and a series of rough tacking duels, the crews exchanged furious invitations to fisticuffs from boat to boat, but once ashore and showered, tempers always cooled and insofar as anyone knows, punch-ups never erupted.

From the outset when the crews started training in October of 1973, the first team asserted itself and by the time *Southern Cross* reached Yanchep, John Bertrand unequivocally maintained that the crew already looked better than the one which sailed *Gretel II* in 1970.

Next to Cuneo, if one had to chose a salient figure aboard *Southern Cross,* it would be the 26-year-old Bertrand. Quiet by nature yet savagely aggressive during a race, he not only has the reputation of being a top level tactician and a well-read student of the subject, but also he is an expert on racing rules and has a heady talent for out-psyching his opponents. His skills as a helmsman, too, are broadly known, making him an ideal assistant to Cuneo in the cockpit of *Southern Cross.* In short, from keeping a trained eye on the rig he designed to actually crewing the boat, Bertrand forms a powerful plus for the entire challenge.

Finally, there remains the incredibly high standards the skipper sets for both himself as well as his crew.

"If he gave a bit of time off to show he cared about the crew, he would get more out of them," one critic declared before promptly contradicting himself by adding, "But after reading what tough, skillful, experienced crewmen and skippers the Americans have, I suppose he is right if he can work his men until they are absolutely

100 percent efficient. It's probably the only way we're going to beat the Americans."

Yet, despite the grind, morale was high at Yanchep and the spirit was incredibly cheerful. If anything, the crew temper soared still higher when *Southern Cross* arrived from her builders, Halvorsen, Morson & Gowland, and the crew had their first real feel of her speed.

"Trygve has built us a very, very fast twelve here," one of them announced quietly with a grin as broad as the Indian Ocean itself.

The only three 12-Meter yachts in the Southern hemisphere, Gretel, Gretel II, *and* Southern Cross.

Alan Bond with some of his crew — with the tension off.

The first aluminum 12-Meter yacht ever built,
Southern Cross *upside down on her builder's floor.*

12

KA4

Of Cloaks and Daggers

THE CLOAK AND DAGGER have been as much a part of America's Cup racing as the cup itself. Secrecy, and the rumors it breeds, have been as natural an element as the sails on the boats. Some of that, no doubt, has been due to man's normal competitiveness, but largely it came about because of the conditions laid down by the *America's* original owners when they turned the cup over to the New York Yacht Club in 1857.

Although the original Deed of Gift went through changes in 1882 and 1887 under the careful pen of George L. Schuyler, then the last man of the *America's* six-man syndicate, as well as having been revised under the eye of the courts in 1956, at no time has there been a change in the syndicate's basic intent of "making it perpetually a Challenge Cup for friendly competition between foreign countries," as the original letter stated so succinctly.

There have been times when the competition was a far cry from friendly and other times when another of the basic conditions was stretched – some said to the limits – on the grounds of friendliness. The latter condition was that the challenging and defending boat each should be designed and built solely in the country of origin. That requirement has called forth for each campaign a heavy concentration on developing new design features, materials and gear that not only would guarantee winning, but also would provide a fillip to national pride in demonstrating clear superiority in yachting.

Such developments, obviously, are closely guarded secrets, although each side does its best to discover what the other has up its sleeve, and the espionage often is of a kind that would make James Bond's 007 look like a credit investigator. Still as each campaign comes down to the first start, the question in everyone's mind is whether the other side really has found a breakthrough that will bring them victory.

Alan Bond, who admits to no relation with James, faced an even worse than usual espionage problem, first because of his determination to start building and training well in advance of the contest which also extended the time for spying, and secondly because his twelve-meter would be the first constructed in aluminum following the decision to permit a change from wood to that modern material in the twelve-meter class.

Even the place where *Southern Cross* was to be built was a hushed secret, although it had been announced that Halvorsen, Morson & Gowland Pty. Ltd., the successors to Lars Halvorsen Sons Pty. Ltd., who had constructed the first *Gretel,* would be the builders. The spy contingent kept a close eye on the Halvorsen shops at Mona Vale, waiting for the first indication that work was under way. They waited in vain.

One enterprising reporter cornered designer Bob Miller, who has a penchant for leading the press astray, in the early Australian winter of 1973 and extracted from him what the reporter and his editors regarded as a prime scoop.

"She's being built under a big hill with grass growing on it," Miller told the reporter solemnly. "It's bombproof . . . and it's press-proof."

Reporters spent days checking out every hill with grass on it for miles around Sydney in the succeeding days while Miller chuckled happily to himself.

In truth, the spot Trygve Halvorsen had picked to build the boat with the approval of Bond and the syndicate was as unlikely as anything that could be found. It was a dreary suburb on the northern edges of Sydney, some forty-five minutes from the center, known as Terry Hills.

Terry Hills originally had been laid out following the end of World War II as a group of small truck farms for rental to returning veterans, but in the years since, it had developed into a collection of ramshackle houses and sheds providing shelter for a variety of small business operations of the kind that live on little but hope and perhaps an idea. Among them, too, were the inevitable collection of catamarans, trimarans and ferrocement dream ships being built by romantic tyros with star-studded dreams of world circumnavigations.

It was not the sort of place anyone would expect to find a professional boatbuilder and even less a grande dame such as an America's Cup contender. But it was there in what appeared to be an erstwhile cow shed set in a patch of trees with all its windows heavily boarded and with dog patrols and armed guards on hand, that *Southern Cross* was laid down.

It wasn't until the Australian spring that the secret came out when a photographer, armed with a telephoto lens, managed to photograph the building with a barn door open to the balmy air. The photograph showed little more than a hazy shape in the darkness — the already plated hull — but it led an eager press to conclude that the contender "was small, simple and fast," although there were those who claimed the adroit Miller himself planted that misleading conclusion in his game of hare-and-hounds with the press.

The fact that *Southern Cross* was to be the first aluminum twelve to be launched only added thrust to the spying, because builders in all corners of the world wondered what changes the Australians would devise with that new material. Not that the Australians were claiming any special expertise, because few aluminum boats had been built in Australia.

In fact, Alan Bond could not be blamed for feeling that the new specifications were simply another elephant pit cut in his path, and one that put Australia at some disadvantage since her knowledge of the art was nearly nil. In the United States, on the other hand, although far from common, aluminum had become something of a trend in the last decade, particularly for the larger ocean racing yachts, and there were any number of yards that had served their apprenticeships in aluminum.

But when Lloyd's was asked to prepare standard aluminum scantlings for the twelve-meter class after the 1970 Cup series by the International Yacht Racing Union, the die was clearly cast and Bond wasted no time. He arranged with the Halvorsens to make a study of the new material which they did, setting up test beds and putting their crews through hours of practice welding and shaping the metal under the eye of technicians from Comalco, the Australian aluminum producers.

Such practice, though, is a long way from the real thing, and in 1972 Bond commissioned Halvorsen to build the 45-foot *Apollo II,* even though *Apollo I* was still a relatively new boat. Bond contended he needed a new boat for the Admiral's Cup series, but Australia's disadvantage was very much in his mind when he asked Miller to design the boat to be built in aluminum, using the same scantlings as were called for in the twelve-meter class. Although *Apollo II* turned out with a few rough spots and somewhat heavier than Miller liked, she did prove fast and she had served her purpose by the time of her launching in

October of 1972, of thoroughly indoctrinating the artisans in the problems of aluminum boatbuilding.

Although boatbuilders by common repute are supposed to be among the world's staunchest conservatives, resisting anything new, it is a reputation they little deserve. In fact, the best of them are quick to try anything new in boatbuilding whether it is a material, a fastening, an adhesive or a new tool. If it works, it is adopted right now. If it doesn't, it is discarded ruthlessly, but most often quietly. And Halvorsen, Morson & Gowland have been considered the best in Australia at the very least, with many claiming they need to bow to none anywhere in the world.

In any event, working in aluminum quickly became second nature and everyone agreed after the launching that *Southern Cross* had gone together with surprising ease. Not that there were no problems, but they were not the kind that could be laid directly to the difficulty of using a new medium. The first holdup that slowed building was when the workers at Sydney's power stations went on strike and power to the dusty cowshed was cut off. Portable generators were rounded up from the odd corners of Sydney, and the welders went back to their tasks. A second major holdup came when *Southern Cross* which, unlike most boats of that size, was built upside down, was framed in and ready for plating.

At that point, the Lloyd's surveyor, who was on hand all through construction to make certain that the standards were observed, noted that the aluminum delivered for the plating was on the ragged edge of meeting the thickness tolerances established by Lloyd's scantlings.

That was a major crisis and all work halted until Brian Leary, the syndicate manager, flew in from Perth with a quick decision.

"We would look stupid if we got to Newport and the other side found we had underweight plating," he decided. "You can be bloody sure we would raise cain if the shoe were on the other foot."

So two weeks dropped out of the building schedule while new plating was rolled to a safe legal tolerance, and then the welders went back to their task with re-doubled intensity.

With her skin finished, *Southern Cross* was rolled over, eased down on her pre-molded lead keel and arrived at that point that every boatbuilder relishes — she began to look like a boat. About the same time, her overall dimensions were checked. They came within a thirty-second to an eighth of an inch of her designs. And the keel, a complex molding job with a dead straight trailing edge, was within fifty pounds of its specified weight. It is rare that any boat comes that closely to her paper image, and indicates precisely the care and skill of her builders.

The builder came by his skill naturally, stemming from a line of Norwegian boatbuilders whose heritage went all the way back to the Vikings and their graceful longboats that even today draw admiration for their lines and construction. The son of Lars Halvorsen, who emigrated to Australia from Norway via South Africa in 1924, Trygve Halvorsen is Australia's most widely known boatbuilder, continuing the business his father started in a small shop in Sydney shortly after he arrived. In those times, there was little demand for boats and the early days in Lars' shop were difficult, but by the time World War II arrived with its flood of government contracts, the Halvorsens had built a well-earned reputation for first class workmanship that carries on undiminished. In 1962 when Australia made its first challenge for the America's Cup with Sir Frank Packer's *Gretel I,* the Halvorsen yard was selected to build her, which they did on the Parramatta River at Ryde near Sydney. A few years later they dissolved the original firm, reforming it as Halvorsen, Morson & Gowland. Trygve calls Trevor Gowland "the finest shipwright in thc world." It was Gowland who actively supervised the building of *Southern Cross* from minute to minute.

It is one of the fascinating anomalies in boating that the people who build boats, seldom sail them — in competition, at least — but there again Trygve Halvorsen is exceptional and ranks with the best sailors in Australia. Nor is it only in the quiet around-the-buoy afternoon races that he shines.

Australia boasts one ocean race that is regarded world wide as the toughest of them all. This is the six hundred mile battle down the Tasman Sea from Sydney to Hobart on the Island of Tasmania which sits astride the Roaring Forties that have pounded and bedevilled sailors since man first went to sea. It is a race that almost always is accompanied by howling gales, mountainous seas and a cold that eats into a sailor's marrow. England's Fastnet, by comparison, is sheer comfort, and America's Bermuda Race, nothing but bliss, so the ocean racing fraternity says.

If anyone can be said to have dominated that gruelling grind, it was Trygve and his brother Magnus. In 1957 they won handily in a boat named *Anitra V*. Again in 1963 in a new boat they designed and built themselves named *Freya,* they came away with the prize. The following year, it was the same. And the year after they did it again for a three-in-a-row record in a major ocean race that has been equalled only by Carleton Mitchell's little yawl *Finisterre* which made a similar three-time sweep of the gentler Bermuda Race at the end of the 1950s. Perhaps far from oddly, both the Halvorsens and Mitchell admitted the only unusual tactic they used in their record wins was to make certain that their boats were being driven to their utmost through the night when most ocean racing crews almost unconsciously ease off a bit and let things ride.

In any case, there is little doubt among ocean racing men in Australia where the Halvorsens stand, even though younger brother, Trygve, at fifty, often is heard talking down the satisfactions of racing and extolling the pleasures of cruising. The racing men urge him on, but they don't quite believe him.

Not that anyone believes there is any deception in the slight, gray-haired Trygve, who speaks so quietly he almost seems shy, because the Halvorsens' reputation for plain, old-fashioned integrity is as widely known and admired as their racing skills.

That integrity early built such a bond of trust between the Halvorsens and the syndicate that when it came time to start the building of the $2,000,000 *Southern Cross,* the start was effected by a simple two-sentence letter which probably is unparalleled for any undertaking of that magnitude. It read:

> Dear Sirs:
>
> Please proceed with the construction of *Australis* (as she was being called then) in accordance with the proposals set out in your letter of 2nd February, 1973. A formal contract will be drawn up pending final clarification of legal and tax matters.
>
> Yours faithfully, B. Leary

Nor was it a misplaced trust because when *Southern Cross* was finally delivered to Yanchep and the bills were totaled, the new twelve-meter had cost Alan Bond just $2000 short of her original estimate. And that in spite of the unforseen and uncontrolable delays such as the power outage and the aluminum plating problem, to say nothing of numerous changes that were made by designer Miller as work progressed, and alterations that were bound to occur as the new Lloyd's scantlings for twelve-meters were put to their first test. Parenthetically, Miller has little use for those scantlings and contends they produce a "flimsy boat that never will be able to go ocean racing like the wooden twelves could."

All told, it was a situation that in most cases anywhere

else in the world would have produced cost overruns not far from the kind the American military establishment seems to enjoy, and that it didn't was a considerable satisfaction to Brian Leary, who mused happily:

"With the contract we started with, anyone else would have taken us to the cleaners. They didn't!"

And Leary knows, because, as syndicate manager, he was the man who watched over every detail of the *Southern Cross* construction and entered it all in a large loose-leaf notebook that he spread out on the vast expanse of his shining desk on the seventeenth floor of International House in Perth. That notebook contained page after page, all foldouts, recording the minutest details of progress — times, dates, materials, suppliers, reasons for delays, problems, solutions, and even an occasional wry comment. It formed an exhaustive log of the birth of *Southern Cross,* but also was almost a hallmark for Brian Leary.

The corrugated iron shed at Terry Hills, N.S.W., where* Southern Cross *was lofted and built.

Master craftsman Trevor Gowland checks the frames.

Plating over the hull under Lloyd's inspection.

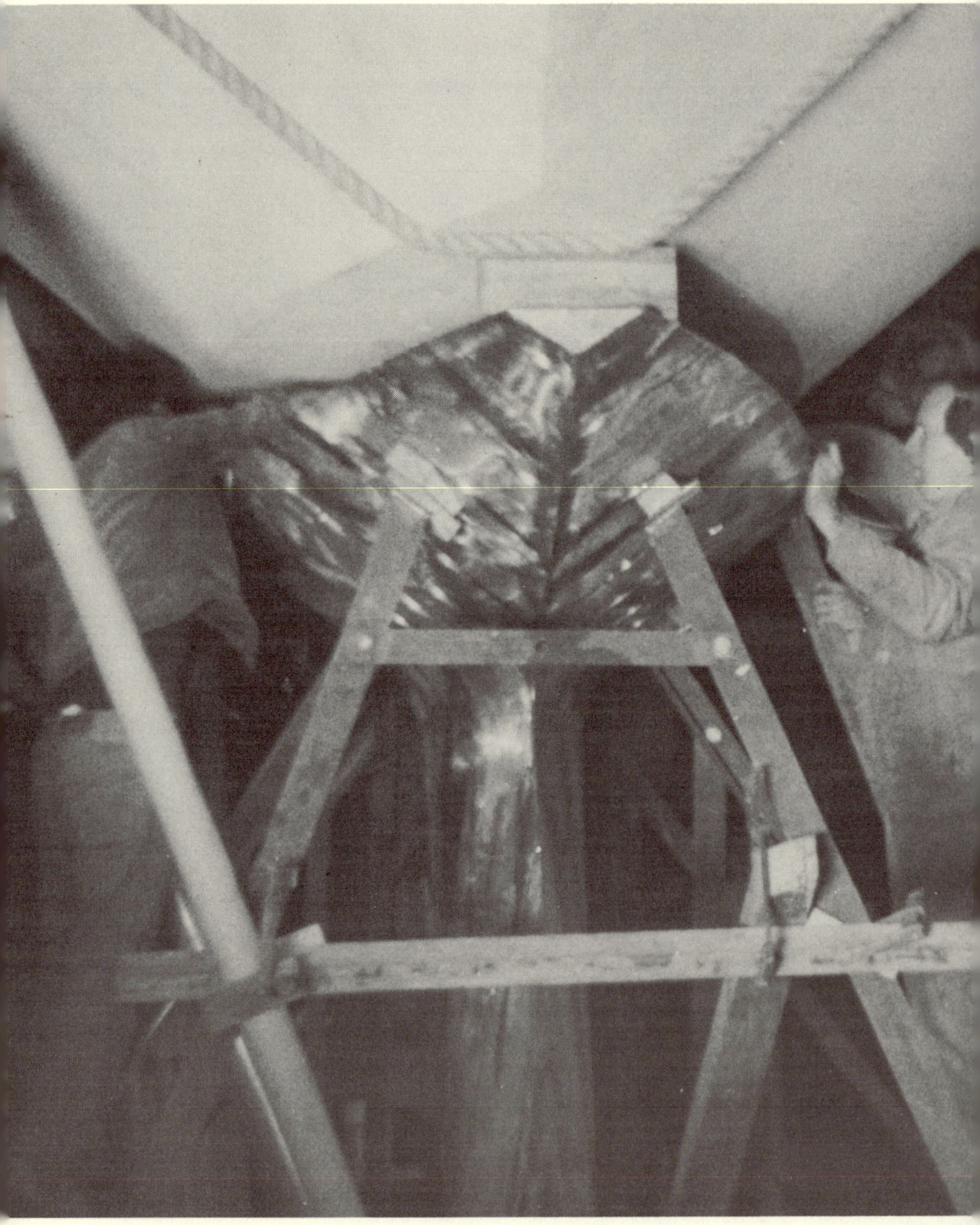

Rightside up, the hull is lowered into position to meet the solid lead ballast keel.

Bond chose Trygve Halvorsen to build Southern Cross. *They raced together in the 1972 Bermuda and Trans-Atlantic races aboard* Apollo.

12

When a stay fitting broke, the mast collapsed.

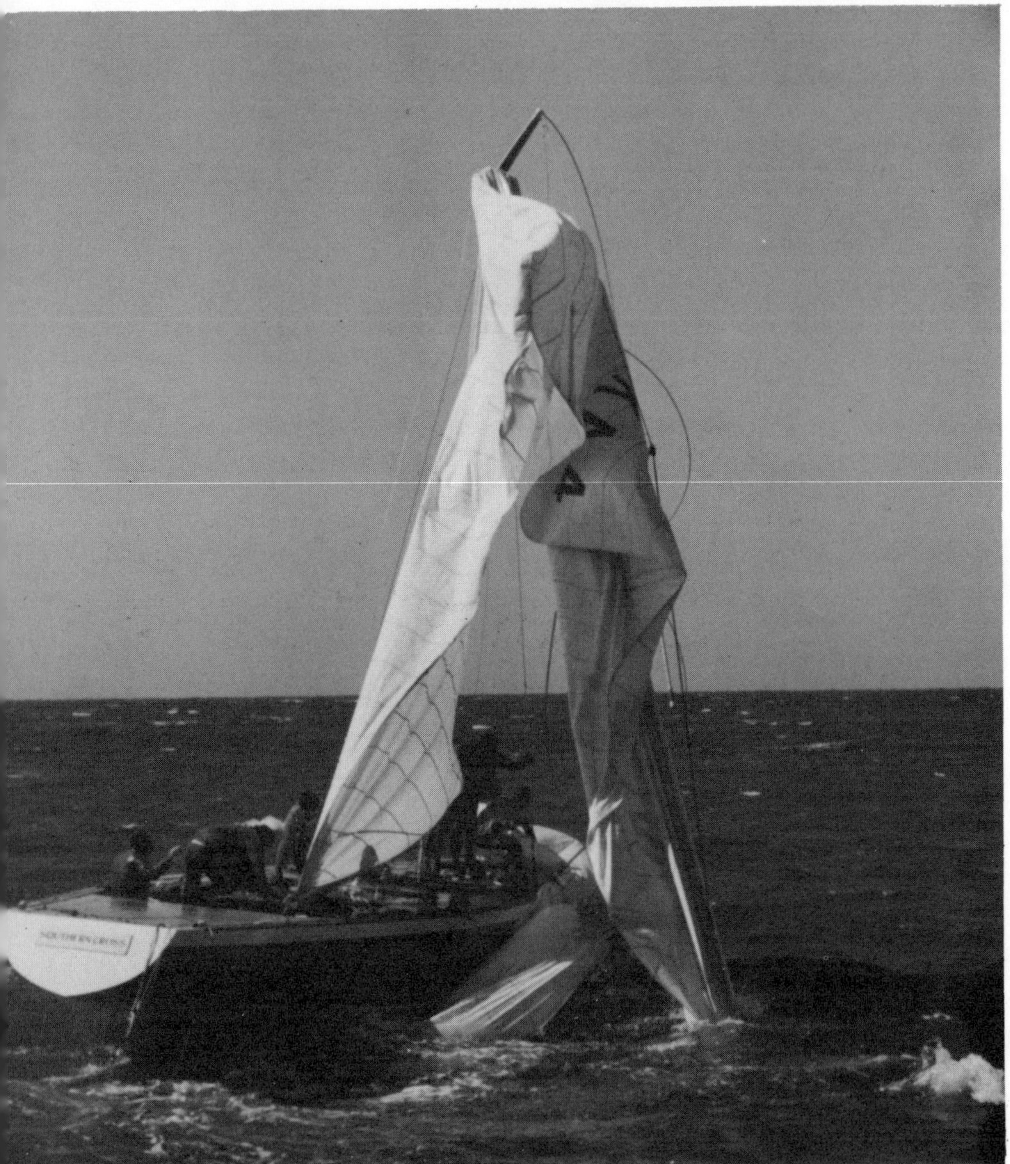

The surprised crew struggled on deck to recover gear

were towed into Yanchep for repairs.

With a hatful of wind, there's no stopping Southern Cross

Southern Cross *points lower than* Gretel II *but foots faster. Holes in afterdeck were added to provide additional ventilation for the crew below.*

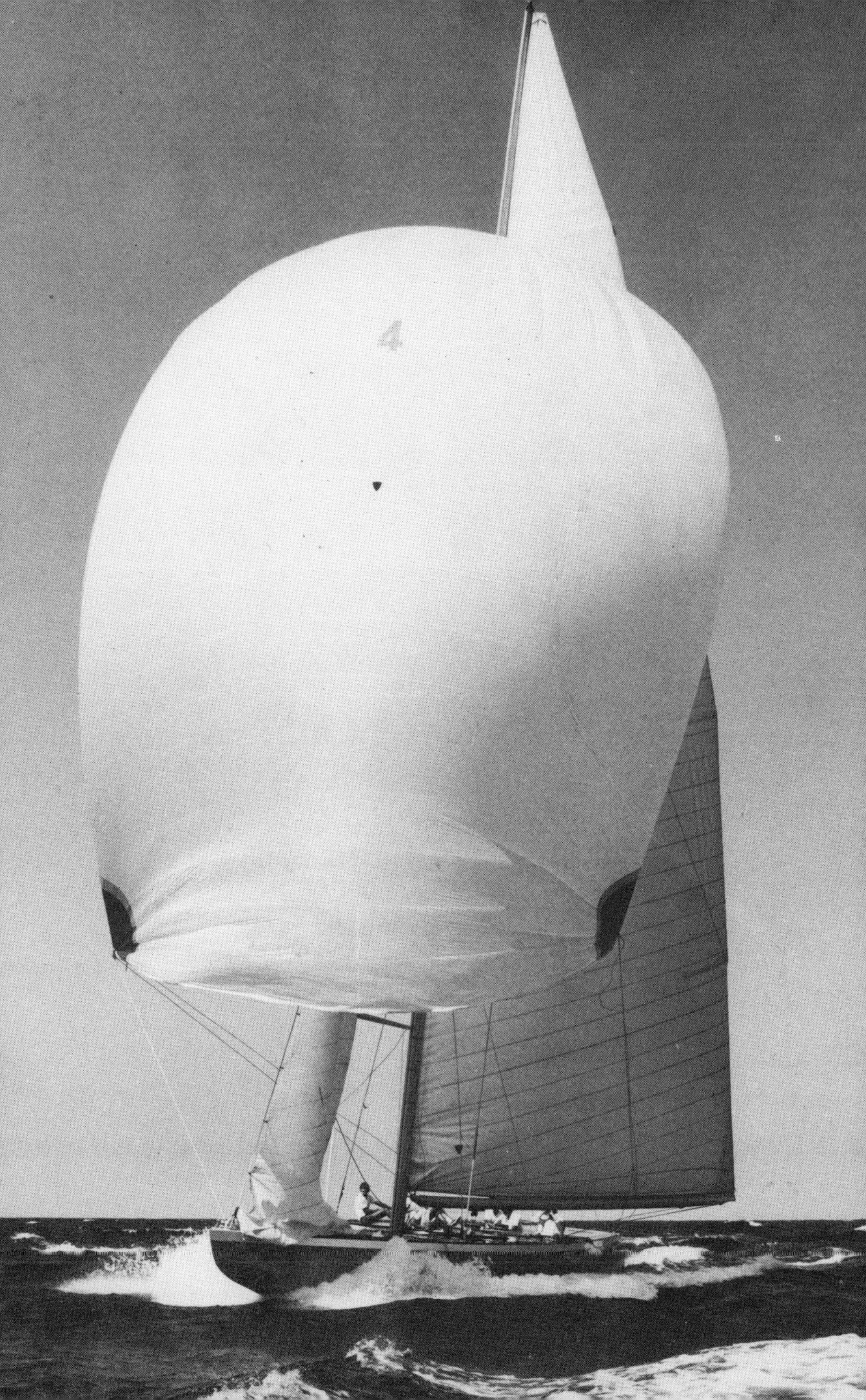
4

12

Old mule Offsider, *with skipper Dave Grundy at the helm, accompanies* Southern Cross *everywhere.*

lender spar and sleek yellow hull add excitement ɔ her speed as Gretel II *is left astern.*

Dapper Brian Leary with Prince Philip.

12
KA4

The Sound of Music

IN BROWN STREET, CLAREMONT, on the fringes of Perth, Brian Leary sat bolt upright on the couch, looking for all the world like Eugene Ormandy conducting Dvorak's *Cello Concerto*. On his lap lay a dinner tray bearing a plate of good Australian ham and whipped potatoes, peppered with shards of raw onion. The potatoes were a Leary specialty. He calls himself a mashed potato connoisseur of world reknown.

Outdoors, the Leary youngsters played in the soft warmth of the Australian summer evening while inside Maxine Leary looked at her husband, his arms still waving above the precisely balanced tray, and wondered aloud if, just for a change, he wouldn't come to the beach with the family the next day for an early morning swim.

It was Christmas. In view of that and after a long pause, he said he would. The answer came hard from a man who, for the last three years, has taken only a day or two away from running Australia's Cup challenge as Australis Syndicate Manager.

"Sometimes late at night, Maxine looks at me sitting there all ready for bed and shakes her head," he recounted in a voice that held a hint of wonderment. "She'll whisper in my ear, 'Hang up! Hang up!', while in the other ear

I have the phone receiver, and a man who is trying to track down a box of bolts."

If the past challenges are any gauge, Leary holds down the single most important post on the *Southern Cross* team. Campaigns in the past failed not so much because of poor skippers, or poor crews, or poor boats — although there were these, too — but because the campaigns lacked a single overall boss to supervise the challenge, to keep track of the minutiae, and to see that everything received a drop of oil when oiling was needed.

Thus when Bond began to lay the groundwork for Australia's America's Cup challenge, he scouted hard for the ideal man to keep a finger on the pulse of what he knew would be a complex proceeding.

"Previous challengers have made a bloody mess of it," Bond once told a Sydney newspaperman. "We are determined to learn from their experience. I hired Brian to handle the Cup campaign because he knows everyone and he is good with people. You have to have someone who will keep people from hitting each other in a project like this."

But as much as a diplomat, Bond knew he needed a man skilled and comfortable with detail and a man who could give more than passing lip service to the ancient refrain that went, for want of a nail, a shoe, a horse, a rider and a battle were lost, because in such campaigns as the challenge, it is the overlooked detail that leads to disaster. Leary, as a talented consulting electrical engineer, well knew that the wrong wire in the wrong place easily could bring a holocaust; he had spent his working life looking for such wires, and avoiding them.

Bond also knew him as a sailor of no mean abilities, having shipped Leary as a member of the crew aboard *Apollo I* in the Sydney-Hobart races, and in the Bermuda and Transatlantic Races in 1970 when the unknowing Romagna had dropped the spark to set off the Australian campaign. It was during the long night watches in a small boat at sea that Bond fathomed the potentials of the intense, galvanic Leary who speaks in trip-hammer time with flashes of hair-trigger humor, and decided that if anyone could pull together the disparate threads of boats, men, ideas, travel, housing, support, morale, food, and social affairs, it would be Leary.

Accordingly, engineer-sailor Leary, who at 44 was the oldest man around, became boss and chief diplomat of the Australis Syndicate with full power to deal with everything from overseeing the construction of *Southern Cross* to finding a ball of proper sail twine, to outlining the pluses and minuses of major policy, and even to blowing a ledge out of the channel.

At the outset of the campaign, Leary drafted an organizational chart for the Australis Syndicate. At the top was the Operating Committee, which consisted of Alan Bond as syndicate chief; Bob Miller, designer, and Brian Leary, syndicate manager. Together the three made all the critical decisions after carefully surveying the elements in think-tank sessions that had no exact schedule but were called as the situation demanded. On Leary's chart, Syndicate Chief Bond was slated to directly supervise Skipper John Cuneo, who in turn had the responsibilities not only for his own crew, but also for sailmakers and riggers as well as *Gretel II's* skipper, Jim Hardy, and his crew. Bond also had listed in his chart box the activities of Bill Lucas who, after he had served his time as sparring helmsman, was to take over the duty of house captain in charge of all social and housekeeping functions at Newport.

Designer Miller's list of tasks went unspecified except for the pregnant notation "boat" and all it implied. It was his duty to evaluate the changes, the additions, subtractions and alterations to *Southern Cross,* to make her, in short, the fastest twelve-meter built.

Under Leary's department came all the rest of the

multiform problems from such abstracts as public relations to specifics like the acquisition and care of the tender for *Southern Cross,* or even the problem of finding a bunk for a visiting fireman.

The frustrations were built in, but few of his problems were more frustrating, Leary recalled, than the question of the Tami-Lift. Moveable lifts are huge, gangling, motorized behemoths that after being driven astraddle a boat can snatch her from the water in slings and easily and quickly carry her to her cradle anywhere ashore. They are common in the United States, but not in Australia. Still, under the specifications of Australian import laws, Leary had to prove to the government that none were made or were available in the country before he could obtain a license to import one. That required letters to every heavy machine manufacturer in the country, and the compilation of their negative replies for submission to the bureaucrats at the capitol in Canberra before a license was issued. In time—a long time—the new Tami-Lift arrived at Yanchep, but as the mechanics assembled it, they found that the essential wheels were missing. They had fallen off a transport truck somewhere in the depths of Pennsylvania, fourteen thousand miles away. Leary went back to the beginning.

One question that normally plagued campaigns for both the offense and defense in the past was no problem to Leary. That was the question of cost. Bond had said at the outset that no effort would be spared, and cost would not be considered. It wasn't.

A long finger of limestone partially blocked the entrance to Yanchep's $1,750,000 marina and one afternoon as she edged into her berth, *Southern Cross* struck it, putting a dent in her keel. The ledge had been a nuisance to the *Gretels* which periodically went aground on their way to their twin moorings deep inside the harbor, but now that the number one boat had fallen victim, the decision was fast.

"Blow it up!" Leary ordered.

"It's going to cost a lot of money," warned the engineer.

"Blow it up," said Leary.

And blow it up, of course, they did.

"You cannot stop doing things because they are expensive," Leary explained.

At the time when all the costs could be totaled, he added, it would be but a small part. There was little question he was right. Mounting an America's Cup campaign from half a world away from Newport could be nothing but expensive. Even such a simple essential as travel expense mounted astronomically. There would be twenty-three crewmen assigned to KA-3, *Gretel II's* official number, and KA-4 — *Southern Cross* — and what with back-up personnel, including lawyers to sort out the legal red tape and protests, there would be at least the cost of forty-four round trip air tickets from Australia to the United States, some $80,000 worth alone.

Since Australians lay great store by the table and in view of meat shortages bedevilling America at times, one of the first items Leary listed on his supplies manifest was twenty-four head of prime Australian beef. No one was to go hungry, nor would he have to adapt himself to the eating peculiarities of another country. They would take it with them. To wash down the steak with native brew the Courage Brewery sent 24,000 cans of its finest from Australia, complete with *Southern Cross* monogrammed cans.

No less a part of the costs would be Chasterlux, the syndicate "camp" while they were at Newport, which Leary had leased early in the proceedings. Although large, Chasterlux is not exactly one of those mastodonian mansions for which Newport is famous. But it is a big stone house, standing at the top of rolling lawns sprinkled with shrubs and shade trees, looking out over the famous Ida Lewis Yacht Club to Fort Adams at the mouth of Newport Harbor and Goat Island beyond. It would be home for the syndicate for the long American summer.

In Newport Harbor itself, *Southern Cross* and *Gretel II* were to be berthed along with their tenders at another well-known Newport landmark, the Newport Shipyard, which has been the base for Cup boats since the races were moved from off New York to Breton Reef, off Newport, in 1930. Nor would that be inexpensive.

As the Australian summer waned, and the American summer began, there was still much uncounted, still much in the guess classification, but few were doubting Bond's estimate that the campaign eventually would cost something more than $4,000,000 in addition to the $2,000,000 that *Southern Cross* had come to. Least of all, Leary.

Leary travelled uncounted hundreds of thousands of miles in his rounds as syndicate manager. While *Southern Cross* was on the stocks, he bounced from Perth to Terry Hills and back again so many times he began to feel, he ruefully admitted, like a tennis ball. And between times, the telephone was seldom far from hand and even more seldom was it out of use. Even so, because a continent separates Perth from Sydney where most of Australia's main suppliers are located, to say nothing of Miller & Whitworth, and Halvorsen, Morson & Gowland, Leary found he had to work on a calendar ten days in advance of anyone else. Deliveries took at least that long, and when things were wanted, they were wanted now, not next week. There were times when Leary cheerfully would have paid a young fortune for a reliable crystal ball.

Nor were all his problems little ones. As the syndicate manager, Leary was as involved as anyone in questions presented by an unaccountable ruling from the New York Yacht Club that the use of so-called "exotic" materials would have to be cleared with the club for either defender or challenger. To some old Cup watchers, that ruling made little sense since the development of new materials and techniques had been one of the greater benefits to come out of America's Cup campaigns, but the club doyens had noted the skyrocketing costs that came with the experiments and contended such astronomical expenses could put a period to the century-and-a-quarter long America's Cup campaigns.

In any case, Leary had prepared Miller's requests to be allowed to use mercury as ballast for *Southern Cross* after the designer had devised a novel plan of a series of tubes to contain the mercury in the ballast area. This would have greatly simplified trimming as well as increasing or decreasing the calculated ballast during *Southern Cross'* sea trials. He also asked about using tungsten which had been used in *Vim's* keel, Australian test borings revealed. *Vim* had been built in 1939 for Commodore Harold S. Vanderbilt — long before the post-war resumption of the Cup campaigns in 1958 — but despite her age, *Vim* had come within a hair of being selected as the 1958 defender with Mosbacher at the helm. The Australians had eagerly chartered her to serve as trial horse for their first challenge, as well as their second and third. Both ballast requests were turned down by the New York Yacht Club.

Not so clear cut was the status of a new material developed in America by E. I. duPont de Nemours & Company, which went under the name of Fiber B. Although a relative of nylon, Fiber B was sufficiently different that the American Federal Trade Commission ruled early in 1974 it would be officially removed from the nylon classification and be given a new generic classification called aramid. Almost without stretch, aramid or Fiber B was under test as a sail material and, according to all rumors, the latest version although subject to sudden ripping performed exceptionally well. If the Americans do use it, Leary said, the Australians will protest it as an exotic material.

The syndicate also was arming itself for another protest if it turned out that the American defender showed signs of having copied some of the highly secret features of *Southern Cross'* underbody. Since *Southern Cross* had been designed and built so far in advance of any of the other Cup boats, and since Alan Payne, designer of the *Gretels,* had been a bit too open with an article he sold to an American yachting magazine, the syndicate charged, they felt that the Australian effort had been compromised unfairly. Leary worried about that, too.

Still another knotty problem was the question of overtraining, a question that besets almost every sporting effort, and one that was of particular consequence to the syndicate since by the time of the final events, the *Southern Cross* crew would have spent almost a solid year of summers in training, all through the Australian summer of 1973 and then the American summer that followed.

"I was lying in bed thinking about it last night," Leary recounted in his office one morning just after Christmas, "when it came to me the answer was that *Gretel II* should get most of the attention now. I can see the situation developing. Right now everyone is happy that *Southern Cross* is going beautifully because they are beating *G-2* pretty easily. But *G-2* is getting the short end. So what? It's like beating a little old lady with a stick."

As he drove to work the next morning in his crimson Alfa Romeo, Leary decided the thing to do was to transfer the emphasis from the new boat to the old. They would get the hard-used, bashed-up *Gretel II* into proper fighting shape at whatever cost.

"She might be up to 95 percent of the speed she had at Newport in 1970 now," he went on. "We don't really know, but if Hardy is given two or three months with his crew, he should be able to get her going through the water a lot faster than she went through it at Newport.

Then, if *Southern Cross* can take her, we will be proving something."

So early in January of 1974, the emphasis went toward polishing *Gretel's* crew to that last notch of skill that sportsmen call the "peak," and continued until the boats left Australia for Newport in April. In the process, lessons were learned in how to fine-tune both boat and crew that would come in more than handy when *Southern Cross* was due her final touches to bring her to her peak in the waters and the weather where she was to fight her real battles.

Such were the mind-snarling problems besetting the syndicate manager, which were over and above his lesser problems. As early as last December, Leary began to work out how big and how many containers would be needed to carry the syndicate's gear to America in April. There had to be room, of course, for *Southern Cross* and for *Gretel II,* and no one would think for a minute of leaving *Offsider,* the tender, at home. *Offsider* probably can lay claim to being one of the most widely traveled small powerboats in the world. The little 35-foot, lapstraked, twin-engined mule had accompanied the Australian challengers in 1962 and again in 1970 as mothership for the *Gretels,* and everyone was certain the twelves themselves would revolt if the rugged little tender was not in her accustomed place at Newport when the battles began.

The freighter herself might cause trouble in view of the worldwide energy crisis. To make certain that the boats kept to their timetable and arrived when they were supposed to, it might mean finding a source of bunker oil for the ship that would carry them. That would be Leary's problem, too.

But Leary had his relief, as well he must. Music accompanied him everywhere. On his not infrequent trips overseas to New York, his first stop was Lincoln Center. He long has been a strong supporter and constant in his attendance at Perth's version of the same. And when it wasn't a formal concert, he had his portable radio tuned to the FM good music station or was listening to his stereo at home. He heartily appreciates to the last nuance those lines that William Congreve wrote almost three centuries ago:

"Music hath charms to soothe the savage beast,
To soften rocks or bend a knotted oak."

And no less soothing to him was sailing. At every opportunity, he took the unused *Gretel I* from her moorings at Yanchep and with a three-man crew picked up on the pier, he would sail casually through the narrow, tricky entrance to watch the fleet and graceful twelves battling on the glittering waters of the Indian Ocean. Invariably, as *Gretel* cleared the harbor, Leary would flick on the portable, and standing deep in the first *Gretel's* cockpit, would soak in the harmony of the sound of music and a spectacle with that far away look in his eyes.

He could not have asked for more, and most often it wasn't until he had once again stepped ashore that he would pause to make such notes as the one to be sure to have the sailmaker's Australian sewing machines fitted with the proper transformers to adapt them to Newport's foreign current.

Such a man is Brian Leary, the syndicate manager, and win or lose, for him Dvorak's *Cello Concerto* will not be far away.

Peter Jackson from Comalco, Bond's public relations counsel Bob Hemery (standing), Syndicate Manager Brian Leary, and Greg Bartel of AMATIL *meet to sign sponsorship agreements.*

A battle among friends. Southern Cross *KA4, with* Gretel *KA1 and* Gretel II *KA3 in easy air.*

12
KA3
KA4

Bow to bow in a practice race as designers Bob Miller and Craig Whitworth study the struggle.

With a starcut bellyful of breeze,
Southern Cross *reaches for the horizon.*

Bound for home, the spinnaker is freed.

Weary and worn, the crew beds down the challenger for another night — and another day of racing.

Home of the challenge, the Royal Perth Yacht Club.

12

KA4

A Plate in the Floor

So THESE WERE THE SINEWS, the money, the minds, the men of Australia's fourth challenge for the America's Cup; each an individual, striving, dedicated and single-minded, but, strangely enough, concerned with a challenge for a Cup that is not a matter for individuals . . . on paper at least.

No individual can challenge in his own name for that most exalted yachting prize, and no individual can ever personally hold it as his own, no matter what it may have cost in money, effort, or heartbreak.

Here again we go back to the first simple letter signed by the *America's* first owners — Commodore John C. Stevens, his brother, Edwin, Hamilton Wilkes, J. Beekman Finley and George L. Schuyler — which turned over the America's Cup to the New York Yacht Club in 1857. Although that straightforward text was replaced in later years by tortured legaleese as lawyers took a hand in protecting the intents of the *America's* syndicate, the conditions always have detailed the syndicate's basic aims. These were most clearly stated in the last paragraph of the original letter, which read:

"It is to be distinctly understood that the Cup is to be the property of the Club, and not of the members thereof, or owners of vessels winning it in a match; and that the condition of keeping it open to be sailed for by yacht clubs of all foreign countries, upon the terms above laid down, shall forever attach to it, thus making it perpetually a Challenge Cup for friendly competition between foreign countries."

There is little chance for any misunderstanding in that statement although it may set some to wondering why anyone would devote time, effort and quantities of money to winning something he couldn't keep. Many have tried to explain it, but perhaps the simplest answer still is, as we have seen, America's Cup fever and all that it implies.

After Alan Bond answered to himself the question of "Why not?" that Vic Romagna had brought on during their confrontation at Newport in 1970, he quietly went to his own club, the Royal Perth Yacht Club, which he had joined when he first acquired *Panamuna,* and proposed his plan. The decision was not difficult for the club since little would be involved for them other than some pleasant paper work, and the reaction was enthusiastic.

For this was a sailor's club and despite its regal title of Royal — a title that has adorned all but one of the nine other clubs that have challenged in the Cup's 123-year history — it is a club of little pretension, but one of intense interest in the arts and skills of sailing. In fact, it may be easier to say not what this cheerful, worthy challenger is like, but what the Royal Perth is not like.

To begin with, unlike the Royal Yacht Squadron at Cowes on England's Isle of Wight, which innocently put the Cup up for competition in 1851 and has tried six times to win it back, the Royal Perth owns no castle with be-ribboned gatekeeper. Neither does it have a tradition of kings and queens and noblesse oblige. Instead, the Royal Perth is a sailor's club where skippers and crews casually gather at the light, airy bar with its view over the Swan River, to re-sail the day's racing over a pint or two. It is a club not of protocol or ceremony, but easy-going informality, of 16-foot skiffs, Sharpies and Solings, and skippers like free-wheeling Bill Lucas, who finished first in the inaugural race to Cape Naturaliste 240 miles southwest of Fremantle as commodore of the Royal Perth in 1955.

Nor is the challenging club like the defending New York Yacht Club. The New York Yacht Club's landbound clubhouse fronts on dreary West Forty-Fourth Street in mid-town Manhattan, almost midway between the Hudson River to the west and the precisely named East River to the east, both out of sight behind serried buildings and skyscrapers. The clubhouse is dim, subdued, unpretentiously grand, but draws something of a ripe nautical air from the finest collection of models and half models of yachts, both famous and obscure, in the world. Among them are exact replicas of all the Cup challengers and defenders, and a large part of the vast collection is displayed in a huge, echoing, high-ceilinged hall called the Model Room. But all through the club in almost every hallway, in every nook, there are other beautifully detailed full models of boats of all sizes that belong or once belonged to members to remind them all of the sea.

In Perth, on the other hand, there are only a few models and a burgee or two gracing the plainly, but comfortably furnished rooms. But neither is there the gloomy gentility looking out on a drab concrete canyon, because the Royal Perth, a ranging cream-painted stucco building of indefinite architecture, sits so close to the edge of the water at a wide elbow of the river known as Matilda Bay, that its doors virtually open on to the piers. Flanking the building to port and starboard are tiers of more piers, all studded with the masts of member's boats, and all awash in the brilliant sun. The club has its own marine railway, and almost every window looks out over some part of sparkling Matilda Bay. There is little to remind the members of the sea inside, but little that can let them forget outside.

And not the least is the Fremantle Doctor, as sailors know the afternoon gale winds that slash in off the Indian Ocean in the summertime as the rapid heating of the vast Australian deserts inland from Perth set off classic on-shore winds. The Fremantle Doctor invariably detects the slightest flaw in either boat or sail, but the Perth sailors take it in stride. It is a memorable experience to stand at the bar with a pint gripped fast, surrounded by sailors still damp from spray, while outside the Fremantle Doctor wields his flashing scalpel in full view.

Unlike the Royal Perth but at the same time of the year, behind the wonderfully baroque facade of the New York Yacht Club, which was patterned after the great stern castles of a Spanish galleon, the members are as insulated from the biting winter gales that roar through the canyons of the city as a bear in his lair. It is only the doorman who keeps a weather eye and then only to warn the members as they gird themselves for their dashes from doorway to taxi or limousine.

Coming in out of the New York weather, though, and up a grand, red-carpeted flight of stairs leading from the marble entrance hall, across another hallway and down another short flight of steps, lies a curtained, softly-lit sanctum with a domed ceiling. In the middle of this small, windowless, crypt-like room that has the feel of a pharaoh's tomb deep inside a pyramid, safely bolted inside a glass case that one may walk around, lies the world's most elusive sailing prize, the America's Cup.

No one today claims that this silver ewer, standing some twenty-seven inches high, is a thing of beauty, but it does have a rococo elegance that comes honestly from the Victorian craftsmen, the London silversmiths R. & S. Gerard, who fashioned it for the Royal Yacht Squadron. No one knows, either, just how much the Yacht Squadron paid for it although it often is said that it was priced at a hundred guineas because the Cup originally had that name. That conclusion, though, is open to some question since at the then current rate of exchange, a hundred guineas would have been about five hundred and twenty-five dollars — the price of a good boat in those days — and as likely the name represents the cash prize that went with the Cup, a common arrangement then.

But whatever the cost or the beauty, the Cup has acquired an almost religious patina for American yachtsmen, so it isn't surprising that Vic Romagna was outraged by Bob Miller's comments on the Cup that day on Derecktor's pier when the seeds of challenge were sown. After boasting it would be a simple matter for the Australians to take the Cup, Miller had added derisively that then they would ". . . toss it out into the middle of Forty-Fourth Street and run over it backward and forwards with a steam roller."

While no one questioned that the bearish Miller was indulging a bit of high-flown hyperbole, still there lurked in Romagna's mind, as in the minds of many American yachtsmen, the question what really would happen to the Cup were America to lose it. Just before the last series in 1970, there had been considerable speculation on the subject, as there has been for almost every series, but enough that the New York Yacht Club felt it was time to draw the lines.

In January of that year, they issued a memorandum speaking squarely to the point under an overline reading "Regarding Future Challenges for the America's Cup."

"Assuming that the New York Yacht Club loses a Match for the Cup," the memorandum posited and then went on:

"Where the Cup is held by a club other than the New York Yacht Club, it is held solely subject to the provisions of the Deed of Gift and the interpretive resolutions in connection therewith, and that club may take action which it deems best in connection with the acceptance of challenges, provided such action is consistent with the terms of the Deed of Gift and the aforesaid interpretative resolutions."

That draws a clear picture, so it is certain that should *Southern Cross* win her campaign, the Cup can not be subjected to the ravages of Miller's steamroller, nor will it grace the mantel in Bond's home any more than it will go to Skipper Cuneo, or Manager Leary, or any other individual. It will be in the care of the Royal Perth Yacht Club in precisely the same way it is in care of the New York Yacht Club today.

The Royal Perth Yacht Club has an entrance hall, too, but it is far from marble or grand. And rising from it is a short, steep doglegged flight of narrow stairs that leads to a recent cupola-like addition to the clubhouse known now as Observation Lounge. It is a fairly small room, again plainly furnished, but it sparkles with sunshine and from its big windows there is a commanding view.

Already this room has become celebrated in Perth, but at the same time it also has become something of an embarrassment to the current Royal Perth commodore, Alan Edwards, who fears that one tiny feature might be construed by the world as a show of Australian cockiness. That feature is a small, stainless steel plate that glints from the middle of the plain green carpet. In it is a hole, bored and threaded, to take the bolt that now secures the America's Cup to its case in the New York Yacht Club.

"Maybe it does seem like counting unhatched chickens," ex-commodore Alan Scott added to the Commodore's apologies, "but we believe in being prepared."

So they do. And so does Bond & Company. Perhaps it is a watchword for sparse, rugged Australia where there still are men who depend on preparation for survival.

But before that little plate could get any use, a long

summer lay ahead of *Southern Cross,* and athwart her course was a sixty-two-and-a-half foot obstacle named *France.* Until she was defeated in the challenger elimination series, the little steel plate in the Royal Perth Yacht Club's new crow's nest would be useful only as a toe catcher.

The plate with a correctly threaded bolt-hole.
The Royal Perth under Commodore Alan Edwards, is ready

*Overlooking the Swan River from Pelican Point,
The Royal Perth Yacht Club enjoys the illustrious
reputation of breeding highly competitive sailors.*

12

This Australian ensign from Sir Frank Packer's 1962 Cup challenge was found aboard Gretel *on her arrival in Fremantle. Brian Leary and Alan Bond wonder if it will bring them luck in 1974.*

Trial horse Gretel II *in the Indian Ocean.*

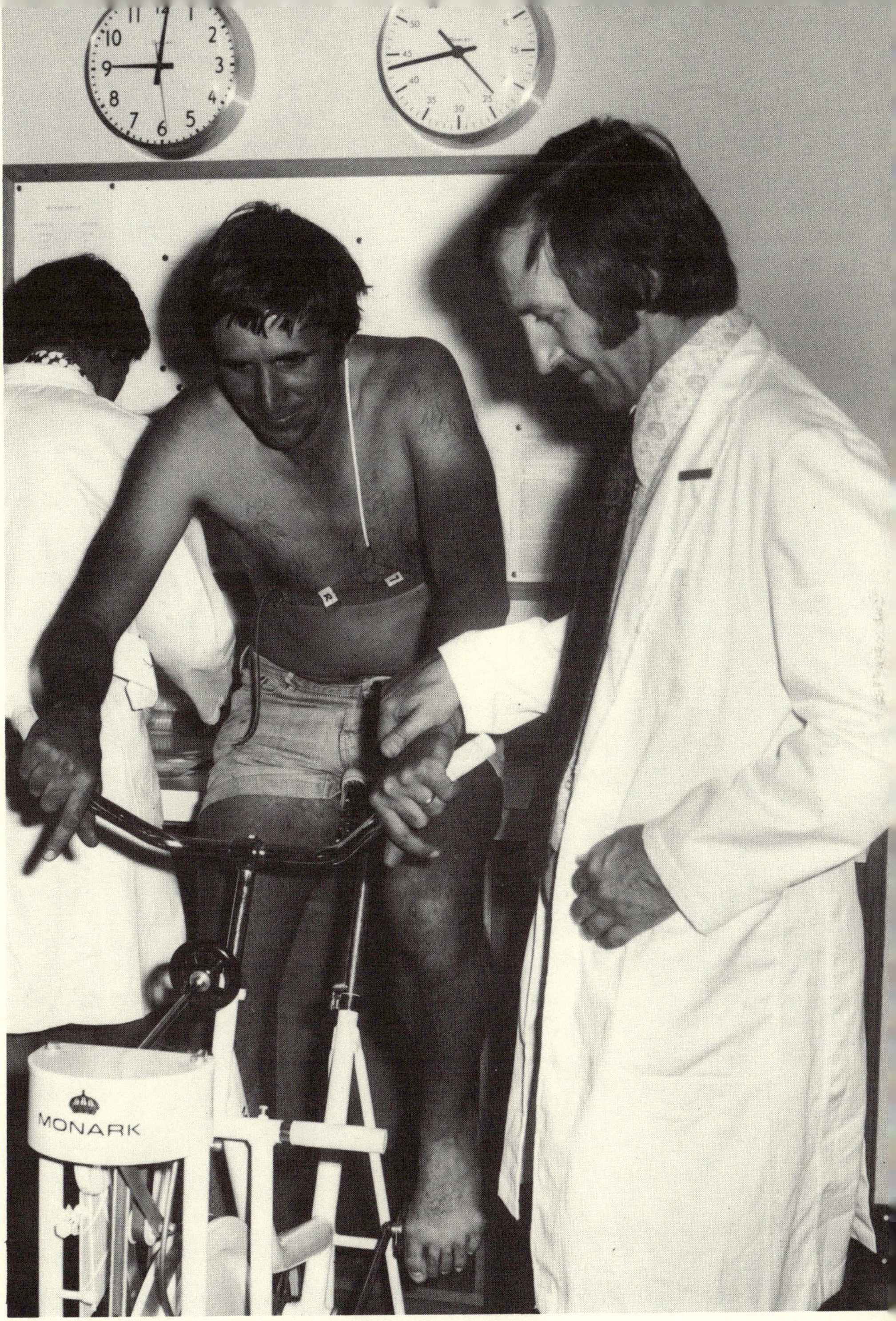

Navigator Jack Baxter is checked over by
Dr. Ken Fitch, Australian Olympic team doctor.

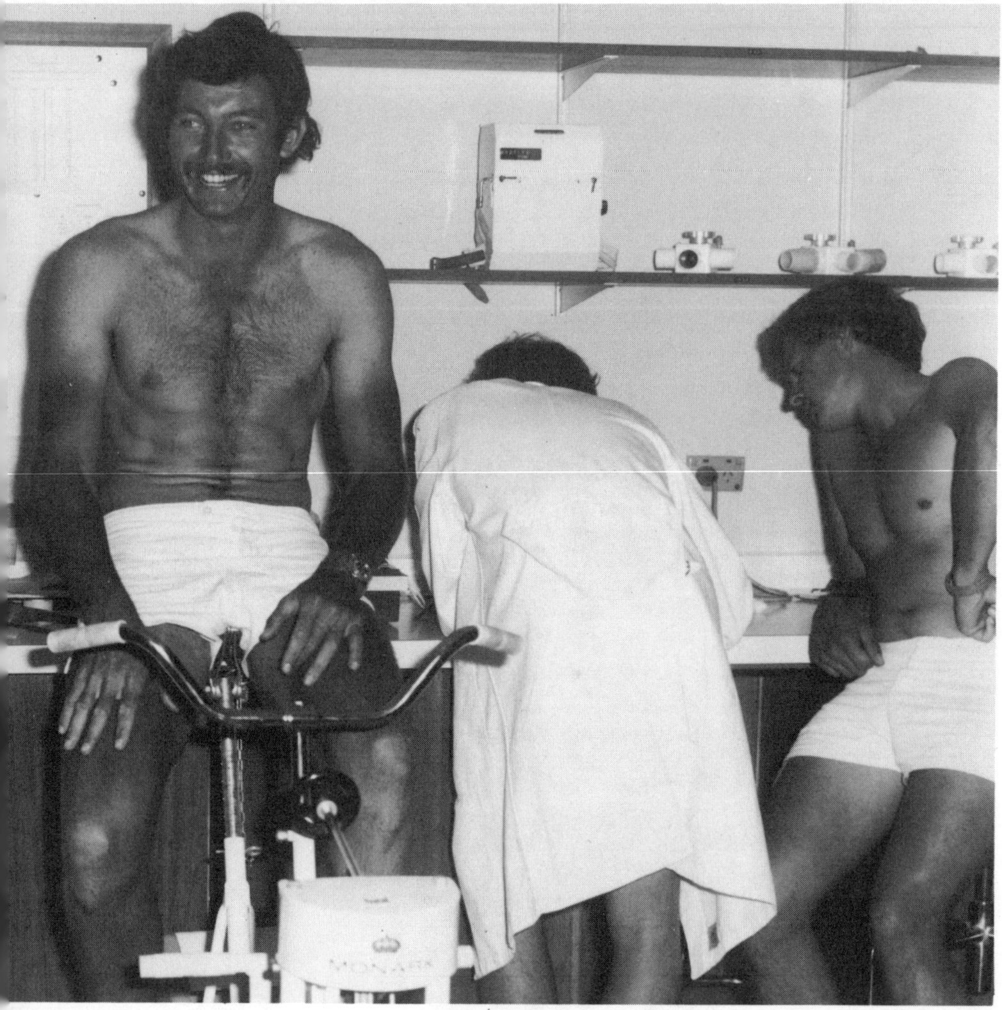

Amiable John Bertrand and young Ron Packer, navigator on Gretel II, *await medical test results.*

Chris Willing blows a lungful for Dr. Alan Morton, from the University of W.A. Physical Education Department.

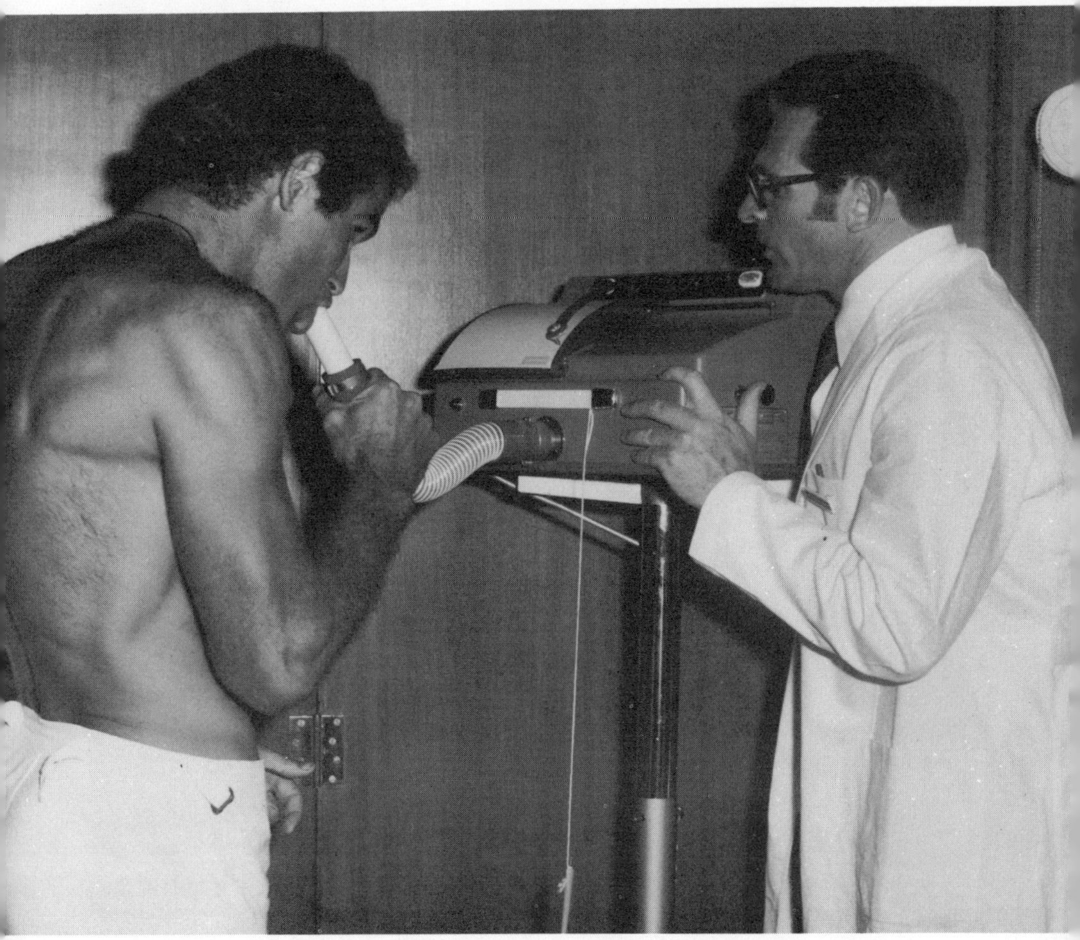

The apple of Bond's eye — the America's Cup.

12
KA4

Still the Others

TAKE ALL THE CONSIDERABLE WEALTH at Alan Bond's disposal. Add all of Bob Miller's art; all the skill at Cuneo's or Hardy's command: all the strength and astuteness in the hearts and minds of the crew, all the organizational talent of Brian Leary . . . add all these together and the sum amounts to the best challenge ever assembled by Australia. But unless *Southern Cross* can vanquish the French and then the American defender, it also may amount to smoke.

The French. If everything had gone according to Baron Marcel Bich's plan, the French well may have rolled over Australians and Americans alike to capture the America's Cup. They had ordered an aluminum boat which, on paper, looked very fast. They had the master himself, Paul Elvstrom, signed as skipper for their challenger. They had past experience to guide them, and they had Bich's ballpoint pen millions to finance their campaign on a lavish scale.

But in Paul Elvstrom lay their greatest wealth. Elvstrom probably is the greatest racing sailor of modern times and comes by the accolade "master" justifiably. Besides an unprecedented four Olympic Gold Medals in single-handed Finns, Elvstrom has won world titles in everything from Five-O-Fives, to Snipes, Stars, Five Point Fives and Solings. And that is only a beginning. His sailing acumen and his concentration on every detail right down to the problems of physical fitness, all are legendary. His only visible problem is one of keeping his head together because he concentrates so fiercely while racing that several times he either blacked out or has cracked under the pressure. Nonetheless, the possibility that the Dane could break the American century-and-a-quarter winning streak and remove the America's Cup from its case, looked very promising. Especially since he had recruited a talented group of Norwegians, Swedes, and Danes to crew for him on the French boat. A lone Frenchman reportedly tried to breach the solid Scandinavian crew list but was repulsed.

If it sounds odd for a French challenger to be manned by a crew of foreigners, it isn't. In truth, it would be a return, in a way, to the early days of Cup competition when challenger and defender alike drew skippers and crews from the ranks of professional seamen, the best of them Scandinavian. None of them were hired on considerations of countries of origin, and that didn't matter. It wasn't until the thirteenth contest in 1920 that amateurs first appeared at the helm when Sir William Burton skippered Lipton's *Shamrock IV* and Commodore Vanderbilt commanded *Resolute*. And it wasn't until the advent of the twelve-meter boats after the post-war resumption of racing in 1958 that amateurs outnumbered the professionals in the crews. There is nothing even now in the Cup conditions specifying crew limitations, so Baron Bich was well within his rights, both legally and historically.

The new aluminum twelve-meter the Baron ordered for Elvstrom was, according to all reports, formidable. Rumors of her shape flew like paper in a Wall Street parade and included a persistent one that her underbody forward resembled the bow sections of a super-tanker.

That suggested she may have had the same bosomly appendage as *Southern Cross.* Her rig looked aerodynamically spotless and her decks were swept clear of fittings, including main winch drums and winches which were bicycled, instead of arm-cranked, below. Another story reported she would use spinnaker launchers which either disgorge spinnakers or swallow them at a gulp. Resembling torpedo tubes, such launchers greatly simplify the normally complicated job of setting or retrieving a spinnaker on small boats, but so far, no one has used them on a boat the size of a twelve-meter.

Another foreigner, the matchless Swiss builder, Herman Egger, would build the new boat at Pontarlier on the French border near Switzerland. As long as the yard was on French soil, it mattered not, like the crew, whether Eggar was Swiss or Sudanese. Egger had built the 1970 French contender *France* and, so rumors had it, the new boat was in frame at the end of 1973. She would be trucked from the Egger yard to Hyères on the Mediterranean for working-up against others of Baron Bich's considerable fleet of twelve-meters — *Constellation, Chancegger* and *France.*

Reputedly, the new boat came from the boards of Andre Mauriac, who had designed *France,* but lending a hand was Elvstrom's close associate, Jan Kjerulf, a young and brilliant Danish designer, who — so it was claimed — ended up more than just lending a hand. In fact, it was said the design was largely his, and when the plans had been handed to Mauriac for signature, the French designer had refused. Whether or not that was the case was a moot question, but the French project for a new boat collapsed just as the fires of public Cup interest again began to blaze for the 1974 contest.

There were other problems, though, that had a bearing. The Baron's fellow countrymen little liked the prospect of being represented by Scandinavians, and said so. Then it was learned that some of the tank testing for the new boat had taken place at Lyngby, near Copenhagen, and the fat was in the fire because the Cup conditions are clear and definite that a challenger must be designed and built completely in the country of her origin. With the threats of protests in the air, Baron Bich made the best of a bad situation by cancelling the new boat and parting company with Elvstrom and his Scandinavian crew.

He did not, however, abandon the challenge. Instead, he reverted to an all-French effort with his old boat *France*. The boat would be French, the crew French and, as skipper, he named Jean-Marie LeGuillou whose nationality was unquestionably French. LeGuillou's chief fame came as skipper of *Cybele,* a Britton Chance-designed Five Point Five with which he won the class championships in 1969, but he also had been Baron Bich's helmsman aboard *France* in 1970 before she left Europe. When the Baron decided to name a co-helmsman, though, LeGuillou elected to stay home instead of travelling to Newport to share the wheel with the 67-year-old Swiss veteran racing sailor, Louis Noverraz. This time LeGuillou hoped to share *France's* helm with no one.

His command was the same *France* that lost four straight races to Australia's *Gretel II* in the first challenger elimination series in 1970. Nor had she been without trouble since then. She sank in sixty feet of water while being towed from Copenhagen to Le Havre in a Force Eight gale in 1972. She had been raised a few weeks later and extensively refurbished and refitted, but whatever facelifting she had undergone, few believed she would be a match for a new aluminum hull.

Even though *France* planned to sail the eliminations against *Southern Cross* as much to store up data for future campaigns as in any real hope of winning, there are those who pointed out that her 1970 failure could be laid mostly to questionable management, and were she placed in the right hands, the representative of the French challenging club, the Circle de la Voile de Paris, could yet be a blue streak.

The English, after a series of stop-and-go projects that were not unlike the Perils of Pauline in their effect on the world's sailors, finally abandoned entering a contender for the challenge, but the Royal Thames Yacht Club, whose original challenge had been accepted by the New York Yacht Club subject to the provisions of conducting the elimination series, set up an international committee to run the elimination series. Headed by Bahamian Robert Symonette, a seasoned Five Point Five skipper and an ocean racing veteran, the committee included A. J. B. Forsyth of Canada, and Professor Ole Westerberg of Sweden. The elimination series, as we already have noted, was a novel departure from Cup tradition in the 1970 match.

But another completely new departure from tradition will be taken under the 1974 conditions for the match with the establishment of an International Protest Committee to judge any violation of sailing rules. In the long history of the Cup, the matter of hearing protests always had been carefully retained by the New York Yacht Club as the sole prerogative of its race committee, and match conditions always had specified there would be no appeal therefrom. Sailors in all corners of the world have compained that this gave the New York Yacht Club an unfair advantage which easily could turn into a despotic whip-hand, particularly if a case came up where the Cup hung on a protest decision.

In truth, protests had been rare in Cup history. In the early years protests were regarded as being on the edge of, if not completely, unsportsmanlike in an era when sportsmanship was pure and highly regarded. There had been no grander gesture in Cup history than one from the Englishman, Sir Richard Sutton, whose challenger *Genesta* was port-tacked and fouled by the defender

Puritan in the 1885 match. The foul had been so blatant that the race committee disqualified *Puritan* on the spot, and advised Sir Richard that all he needed to do under the match conditions was sail over the course to take that race, which he could have done despite a splintered bowsprit. Sir Richard gallantly declined the suggestion with the shouted comment:

"We didn't come to win that way."

Times, though, have changed and in this age of deceit, this age where "the nice guy comes last," protests are quite another matter and are used as an essential part of racing tactics. Whether or not they fit a philosophy of true sportsmanship is a question that has been pushed carefully under the rug. In any event, it is a different climate, and the inevitable results surfaced in the last Cup contest when *Gretel II* and *Intrepid* collided at the start of the second race which *Gretel* went on to win, albeit with protest flags flying on both boats. The New York Yacht Club Race Committee heard the protest and ruled against the Australian boat, reversing her win to a loss, in a decision that today most sailors consider was proper.

But the press, both in America and abroad, descended on the New York club and belabored them for their position as judge, jury and executioner, and the club later announced quietly that in the future, America's Cup protests would be heard by an international protest jury with the 1974 jury to be formed by the International Yacht Racing Union's president, Beppe Croce of Italy. It is a significant departure from Cup contests of yore.

As defender for 1974, the New York Yacht Club will pick from something old in wood, something not so old in wood, and a pair of aluminum newcomers. The old boat is the Olin Stephens-designed *Intrepid* which, other than the first *Columbia* in 1899 and again in 1901, was the only defender ever selected to defend the Cup twice. She had no trouble trouncing *Dame Pattie* in 1967 with

Bus Mosbacher in command, then, having undergone extensive alterations designed by Britton Chance, she won again under the command of Bill Ficker in 1970. To be sure, she is wooden and therefore automatically dated, but the wooden twelves still may use exotic materials forbidden to aluminum twelves and with a new keel, reshaped rudder, and fined down stern sections drawn by Olin Stephens and executed by Gerry Driscoll's Custom Boatyard in San Diego, the new-old *Intrepid* cannot be counted out.

A skilled crew of West Coast sailors will man her, led by boat-builder Driscoll as skipper. In the past, Driscoll has won back-to-back Congressional Cups together with a bagfull of trophies in other classes. With Driscoll in *Intrepid's* cockpit will be world Star Class champion Bill Buchan of Seattle as stand-by helmsman, and John Marshall, a bronze-medal winning crewman in Dragons in the Olympic series won by John Cuneo in 1972. Marshall, a sailmaker, will act as sail trim expert.

Intrepid will sail under the aegis of a publicly funded, tax-deductible foundation, the Seattle Sailing Foundation of Seattle, Washington, which marks still another novel departure from history in America's Cup contests. In all the twenty-one contests through 1970, the uncounted millions of dollars expended on contenders and defenders and their campaigns in the United States have been put up by men who expected, and received, nothing for their money other than being listed on the syndicate rosters and, often, even those went unpublished or obscurely published at best. Despite petitions, the Internal Revenue Department turned a cold ear to requests for at least some tax relief, contending the Cup contests were simply a pleasure to syndicate contributors and no more deductible than a garden party. But in view of the obvious fact that the Cup defenses were more than that; indeed, they have been matters of national pride and concern, and in view of spreading discontent, the Revenue Department reversed itself in mid-1971 when they granted a tax-exempt status to a California group called the California International Sailing Association which had planned a contender for the Cup defense in 1974. While CISA's plans never matured, the ruling opened the door for tax-exempt foundation financing, and the Seattle group was a result as well as the mounting of a double-strength campaign by a group working through the Kings Point Fund of the United States Merchant Marine Academy at Kings Point, New York, on a tax-deductible basis.

The Kings Point group acquired an enigma named *Valiant* which is the semi-old wooden twelve-meter in the current series. While steered by Bob McCullough in 1970, *Valiant* — then Olin Stephens' latest twelve-meter — never came to life. Steering was difficult; she threw a small and unatural feather of water from her weather quarter; critics blamed Stephens for giving her poor stern lines. Altogether, this possibly quick twelve-meter misbehaved like a spoiled child and no matter how they fussed and fumed over her, *Valiant* refused to respond.

After the end of the 1970 contest, the syndicate donated *Valiant* to Skipper McCullough's alma mater, Brown University, which didn't seem to have much educational effect on her manners, and later on she was passed along to the Merchant Marine Academy and the Kings Point Fund. There she came under Britton Chance's control and he took his turn at trying to correct her problems by altering her ballast and straightening out a balky steering system, the idea being to employ *Valiant* as a trial horse for *Mariner,* a new Chance boat designed in aluminum which will be the Kings Point group's main thrust in the 1974 contest for the defense.

If Chance has fixed *Valiant,* she finally may discover the life she has been skirting for so long. If he hasn't, it won't be the fault of George Hinman, her skipper. Hinman is a man who knows how to milk performance from hulls long given up for dry, a skill he demonstrated in 1970 when he sailed the cast-off *Weatherly* so cleverly he gave more than one of the new twelve-meters nightmares in light air.

Yet despite the traditional virtues of wood, it is unlikely the vintage boats will hold off their new aluminum sisters for long. The aluminum twelves are lighter; designers are able to arrange their ballast to better advantage, and some say they tend to hobby-horse less. Moreover, should drastic surgery be necessary to correct a problem, it is merely a matter of wheeling out the cutting torch and replacing the faulty part with a pre-fabricated new part . . . a question of days, not weeks as it is with wood. It is not so much that aluminum as a material is superior to wood, it is simply that the new boats will be aluminum and therefore, as Olin Stephens contends, a reflection of the latest thinking in design.

The biggest problem confronting the third defense syndicate in 1974 was cash. The Courageous Syndicate was particularly hard hit because, unlike the other two, that syndicate enjoyed no tax-deductible status. Thus in December 1973 with gasoline evaporating, oil going back underground and the stock market plunging, the Courageous Syndicate asked the New York Yacht Club to postpone the Cup races for another year until 1975. Far behind in its fund-raising campaign, the syndicate claimed they could not afford to build or campaign *Courageous*. But the New York Yacht Club turned an unsympathetic ear, and the syndicate announced cancellation of its plans to build its boat.

With that turn in events, Bill Ficker, the successful 1970 *Intrepid* skipper, who was returning to combat with tactician Steve Van Dyck and navigator Peter Wilson in the new boat, made other arrangements for his summer. No sooner was Ficker's summer planned than the Courageous Syndicate changed course again 180 degrees and announced it would resume building the contender after all. Ficker was replaced by Bob Bavier, who sailed *Constellation* to four straight wins over the British *Sovereign* in 1964, and soon afterwards the syndicate lost Van Dyck and navigator Wilson. The afterguard's transfusion was completed when Halsey Herreshoff — great grandson of the Wizard of Bristol, the incomparable Nathanael Herreshoff, who designed and built five successful Cup defenders from 1893 through 1920 — came aboard as navigator and Jack Sutphen joined to handle tactics.

But even as the blood dried and builders plated the revived *Courageous,* the syndicate still lacked funds. Yet, with the hull nearing completion at Minneford's Yard on City Island within sight of downtown New York, it seemed unlikely the syndicate would withdraw again. Somehow they would find the money somewhere.

Surprisingly, the one man who stood to gain in reputation, at least, by *Courageous'* near demise in 1973 was young Chance. It was Chance, though, who seemed happiest when the Courageous Syndicate changed its mind and said it would continue to build Olin Stephens' latest twelve-meter. With that decision, instead of facing the dated *Intrepid, Mariner* would meet a new aluminum boat for the right to defend the Cup.

The reason Chance eagerly looked forward to this engagement goes back to 1970 when he was commissioned to redesign *Intrepid,* whose lines originally were conceived by Olin Stephens. The altered *Intrepid* proceeded to win the trials and went on to keep the Cup for the New York Yacht Club. But, perhaps naturally, it was claimed in some quarters that *Intrepid* still bore the Stephens' mark and that Chance's only contribution had been to slow her in light air. Accordingly, Chance longed for the day when a brand new twelve all of his own design would meet Stephens' brand new twelve to settle the score.

"I'm very disappointed," Chance had said when the Courageous Syndicate announced its withdrawal last winter, "I wanted a clean shot at Olin and now I've missed it."

But, of course, he didn't. Chance's boat *Mariner* was built amid airtight security at Bob Derecktor's yard in Mamaroneck. Derecktor, himself, was signed to sail aboard *Mariner* but, in consideration of his age, he was scheduled to serve as a lowly winch tailer. Still, Derecktor probably has sailed more miles than anyone aboard *Mariner* and as a sailor's sailor, it would be hard to believe he won't be the most useful man aboard.

At *Mariner's* helm will be 35-year-old Ted Turner from Atlanta, Georgia. As the ex-owner of *American Eagle,* a Cup boat contender turned ocean racer, Turner has logged countless hours and sailed numberless miles of ocean at the wheel of a twelve-meter. While that may have little effect on his match-racing skill, it should provide a matchless advantage in acquiring a feel for the sensitive twelves. With *American Eagle,* he won the World Championship of Ocean Racing, Florida's Southern Circuit, the most prestigious free-for-all in ocean racing. He took the Sydney-Hobart on corrected as well as elapsed time, the Annapolis-Newport, and other titles too numerous to recount. In her day, *American Eagle* with Turner in command was the most feared boat in ocean racing.

In addition to his many *American Eagle* successes, Ted Tùrner won every major title put up by the Five Point Five meter class when that class was at its zenith some time ago.

Sharing *Mariner's* cockpit with Turner will be Dennis Connor, a young Star Class champion and 1973 winner of the Congressional Cup series which John Cuneo lost so badly. Also in the cockpit will be Robbie Doyle, an even younger small boat expert with a keen enough eye to spot the most microscopic flaw in any sail.

How well the *Mariner* team works together was indicated last winter. Turner took most of his crew to Florida where they sailed in the North American One Ton Championships for, as Turner puts it, "a bit of practice." Despite sailing the borrowed ocean racer *Robin* against the unrelieved pressure of the best One Ton fleet ever assembled in American waters, Turner won. It isn't often that a drill turns into victory.

Turner and the Australians are old shipmates. Bob Miller sailed with Turner when *American Eagle* won the Sydney-Hobart, and Turner has known Bond all around the world. They are alike in many respects. They are both in their thirties. They share an aggressive, hold-on-tight, never-say-die, go-for-broke attitude towards winning. And they are close enough that at one point Bond agreed to exchange a piece of property at Yanchep Sun City for shares in one of Turner's Atlanta television stations.

Bond will be at Newport as owner of *Southern Cross*. Turner will be in command of *Mariner*. Yet there is little doubt that their effect on each other will be profound should the two boats meet in the Cup matches. On one thing they both agree, though — the sun will be brighter without Elvstrom casting his long shadow over the wharves at Newport.

Barring depression, holocaust, and other catastrophes, by October the men and the boats racing in the 1974 campaign will be a part of the America's Cup history. The alumnium boats will have shown or not shown their superiority to the wooden hulls. The underbodies of the new American twelve-meters will have been examined and analyzed by as many experts and more as already have sighted along the underbody of *Southern Cross*. The hulls will have been compared, cross checked and pried apart by eye. The trials to pick the American defender will be over, the eliminations between *France* and *Southern Cross* done.

And as the fogs of autumn start to roll across Brenton Reef and spring comes to Yanchep 12,000 miles away under the Southern Cross, the Cup will be won.

No challenger could come a greater distance.

Southern Cross, *reaching for her reward.*

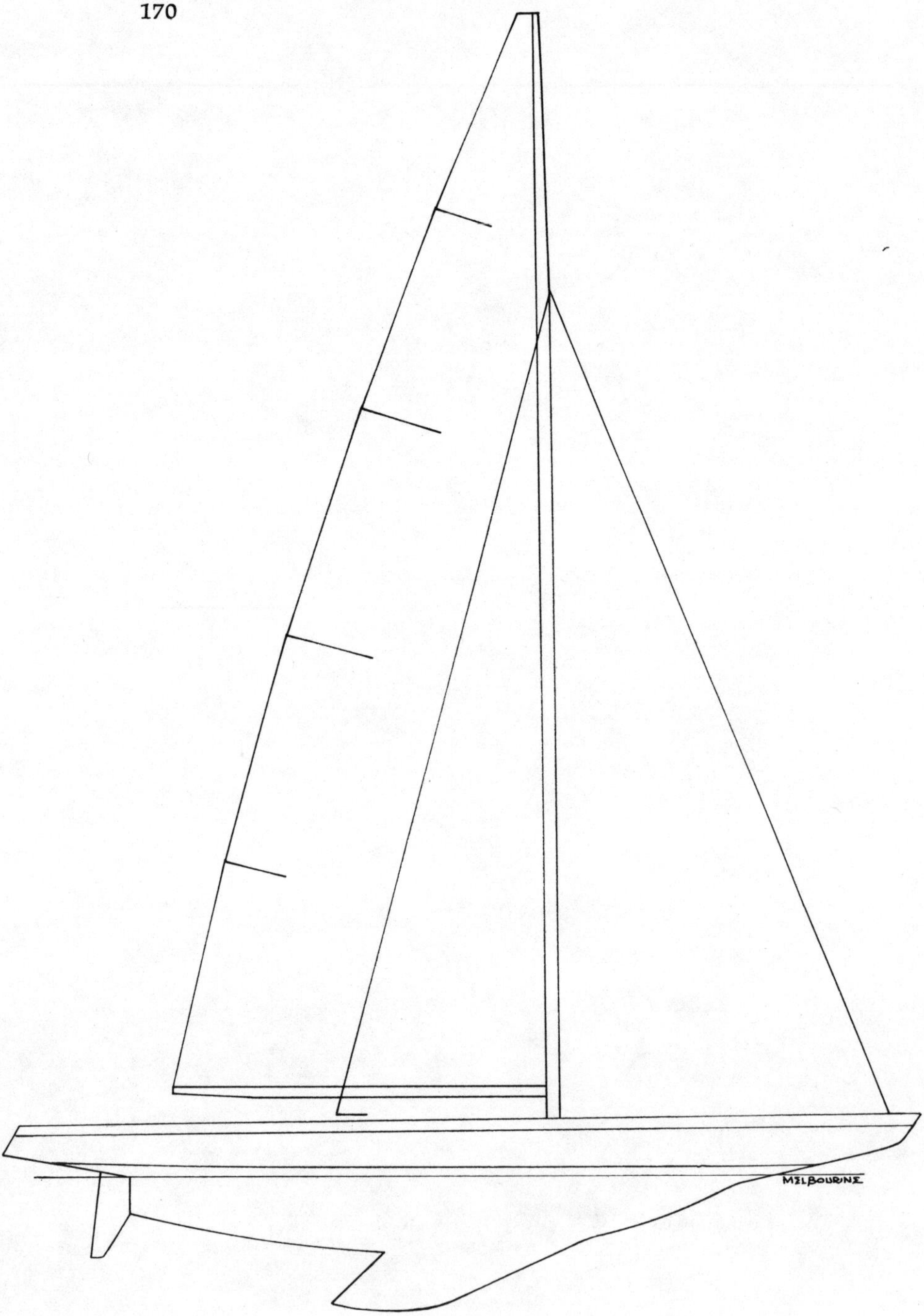
MELBOURNE

Specifications for 12 Meter yacht

SOUTHERN CROSS

Length on deck	65′ 10″
Length over all	67′ 3″
Length on waterline	46′ 8″
Overhang forward	10′ 9″
Overhang aft	9′ 10″
Extreme beam	12′ 4″
Draft	9′ 6″
Weight of ballast keel	55,000 lbs.
Total displacement	62,000 lbs.
Height of mast above deck	80′ 8″
Mainsail	foot 27′1″ luff 80′1″
Spinnaker	foot, luff & leach 60′
Genoa (max.)	foot 39′9″ overlap 15′9″
Measured sail area	1811 sq. ft.

BASIC TWELVE-METER FORMULA

The Twelve-Meter Class of racing sailboats is based on a quotient of the following formula that equals 12 meters,or 39.37 feet.

$$R = \frac{L + 2d + SA - F}{2.37}$$

R = Rating (12 meters in this class) .

L = Length of the hull measured approximately 7 inches above the load waterline. Corrections for girth are applied to this measurement.

D = The skin girth is measured on the surface of the hull from sheer to keel about amidships. The chain girth measured at the same place is the length of line stretched taut from the sheer to the keel and is deducted from the skin girth to give the D component.

SA = Sail area includes the mainsail and the fore triangle bounded by the mast, forestay, and deck.

F = Freeboard, or height of hull above waterline.

2.37 = The mathematical constant.

PHOTO CREDITS THE SUNDAY TIMES, PERTH: 2, 28, 31, 93, 136. ILLUSTRATIONS PTY. LTD: 27, 172. WEST AUSTRALIAN NEWSPAPERS LTD: 14, 29, 30, 70, 84, 109, 115, 124, 173. NEWS LIMITED, SYDNEY: 148. INDEPENDENT, PERTH: 15, 16, 20, 65, 130-1. A. J. NUTT & ASSOCIATES: 32, 44, 45, 46, 129, 138, 145, 146-7, 150, 151, 152, 153. AUSTRALIAN INFORMATION SERVICE: 52.

MELBOURNE SMITH, *design and production.*
VICTOR JORGENSEN, *editorial.*
SERVICE COMPOSITION COMPANY, *typesetting.*
KINGSPORT PRESS, INC., *printing and binding.*